Revealing Life Insurance Secrets

How the Pros Pick, Design, and Evaluate Their Own Policies

Richard M. Weber, MBA, CLU

Marketplace Books
Columbia, Maryland

This book, along with other books, is available at discounts that make it realistic to provide it as a gift to your customers, clients, and staff. For more information on these long lasting, cost effective premiums, please call us at (800) 272-2855 or you may email us at sales@traderslibrary.com.

ISBN 1-59280-174-9

Printed in the United States of America.

Contents

Foreword

As a Certified Public Account and tax attorney, I am frequently asked by my clients about life insurance: Do I need it? Do I have the right kind? How does my policy "stack up" against what's available? I know that, in part, they ask me these questions because they perceive my advice to be both educated and independent of the insurance sale.

Before the introduction of such high-tech policies as Universal and Variable Universal Life, providing answers to my clients was fairly easy. But as the insurance industry has brought newer, more flexible types of life insurance into the marketplace, my responses have been more difficult to contemplate. Even within my own personal policies I'm confronted with the disturbing question: How is it that a quoted premium isn't really an amount I can rely on to maintain the policy for as long as I live? Can I rely on a policy illustration that disclaims any predictability or reliability?

This book provides the answers in language that – for an insurance guy – is reasonable both for advisors and their clients. Dick Weber has devoted the last 20 years of his insurance career to putting himself in the client's shoes, devising communication processes and even software to give the consumer an opportunity to make sense of it all.

The title really says it all: "Revealing Life Insurance Secrets: How the Pros Pick, Design and Evaluate Their Own Policies." Life insurance *is* complicated, unnecessarily so given that it's an important part of family, estate, business, and charitable planning. For most of us, life insurance is something that we need to seriously consider and understand at one time or another in our financial lives.

In my experience as a tax and financial planner, I want to understand how something *works* and to make sure I understand it. Many of my clients do *not* want that same level of understanding as long as they believe my utmost consideration is helping them with their concerns and questions. Dick's breakthrough was in developing statistical analyses that provide a better ongoing measuring tool of how likely a policy would sustain for as long as the client might live. The benefit of this process is given credibility in its recent confirmation by federal securities regulators, and this information makes it easier for me to counsel my planning clients.

Perhaps of utmost concern to readers is the consideration of life insurance that's already been purchased. Trillions of dollars of life insurance have been bought in the last 20 years, and a significant amount of that insurance is the kind where premiums are not fixed but must be managed for changing economic conditions. A Universal Life policy purchased in 1985 with a 10 percent crediting rate is now crediting just 4 percent; that doesn't make it a bad policy, it's just that things have changed, *and perhaps expectations have not been effectively managed.* If a funding premium was calculated using 10 percent and *not* adjusted for the reality of falling interest rates, that policy is likely to fail. A similar result is waiting for owners of Variable Universal Life whose funding premiums were calculated in the "dot com" surge. This book moves beyond blame and gives policy owners solid, credible advice for managing these policies.

When it comes to understanding life insurance, I've looked to Dick Weber for more than 15 years for that expertise and clarity of communication.

I'm glad he's now willing to share it!

Martin J. Satinsky, CPA/PFS, J.D., LL.M.
Partner, Tax Services
Smart and Associates, LLP
Devon, PA

Introduction

My name is Dick and I'm a recovering life insurance agent.

I've been licensed to sell life insurance for more than 38 years, but in the last 12 years found that I preferred spending my time advocating for better consumer information and disclosure. I've worked with life insurance companies, Broker-Dealers, and insurance agents to foster better processes the consumer can use to determine such things as: How much life insurance do I need? What kind of policy best fits my needs? How much should I expect to pay for life insurance? And, with which life insurance company should I "partner" for a policy I fully expect to own for 40 or 50 years? More recently, we've begun to focus on whether old policies should be replaced with new ones.

Life insurance is an extraordinary financial tool and the only way I know to affordably deliver resources to just the right person at just the right time of financial stress – loss of income, taxes, or other liquidity needs due to death. As simple as life insurance should be, it's become complicated by both psychological factors (who really wants to consider their own death?) and a reflection of the increased complexity in all financial decisions and products that can potentially serve our needs.

In the universe (you'll pardon the pun) of life insurance knowledge, there's infinitely more that's *not* included here. This book is my humble attempt to focus on the things financial advisors and their clients really need to know about making life insurance decisions that are in the best interest of those clients (and in turn their beneficiaries). In order to make it useful for today's high-tech life insurance policies, I've had to leave such important subjects as annuities for another time.

The wisdom contained in this book is not mine alone, but derives from a career-long collaboration with such industry luminaries (to name just a few) as Guy Baker, Ben Baldwin, Steve Leimberg, Alan Press, Joe Belth, and my early mentor, retired actuary Walt Miller. Special acknowledgement is also owed to the Society of Financial Service Professionals, which in 1992 took the brave step of introducing the Illustration Questionnaire to the life insurance industry – and insisting that life insurance companies substantially increase disclosure and training to their agents and brokers about the difference between sales illustrations and the policies they represent.

Section 1

Understanding Modern Life Insurance Policies

Chapter 1

Not Your
Father's Oldsmobile

As is typical between generations, it's easier to note differences than similarities. And there is a striking difference between the life insurance needs and products available in the 1950s and those in use today. In the 1954 television series introduction of *Father Knows Best*, Robert Young and Jane Wyatt exemplified the best of American family life in the quiet period between the end of the Korean conflict and the arrival of the Beatles. Intriguingly, Young's character of Jim Anderson worked as a life insurance agent; the producers thought such a career would give him respectability and plenty of time at home. His middle-class male clients earned perhaps $8,000 a year (single-income families dominated America in the 1950s; mothers rarely worked outside the home) and satisfied their need to protect loved ones from loss of income because of premature death with $5,000 and $10,000 Whole Life policies. Total life insurance for such a family rarely exceeded $25,000. After all, homes in many parts of the country cost as little as $5,000–$10,000, a new Oldsmobile was less than $3,000 in 1955 (and the gas to power it was 20–25 cents a gallon), and candy bars were 5 cents. The prime lending rate was 3.25 percent,[1] mortgage rates were typically 4 percent (and often obtained from a life insurance company), and passbook savings rates were 2 percent. Whole Life insurance was a reasonable purchase with a long-term rate of return on cash value that was at least as good as a savings account.

Fifty years ago, life insurance was a staple of middle-class America. Policies were almost always tucked away in a drawer with other important documents and rarely looked at until death occurred and a claim was submitted to the insurer. Life insurance companies were the backbone of the American economy in the 1950s, providing home mortgages and policies that represented a portion of the typical family's savings. With $63 billion in assets by late 1950, the life insurance industry was second only to commercial banks' $148 billion in financial institution total assets; the next closest industry was mutual savings banks with $22 billion. At that time, the mutual fund industry barely existed.[2]

Baby boomers growing up in the 1950s may have an almost cinematic, nostalgic recollection of an era tame in inflation yet booming with postwar economic expansion. The guns-and-butter conundrum of the Vietnam conflict, however, soon created a long-building pressure on inflation and thus interest rates. By 1971 inflation had briefly exceeded 6 percent, and the trend was thought to be so dangerous to the economy that President Nixon imposed wage and price controls in an attempt to head off the combination of rising costs and a stagnant economy. In spite of such efforts, inflation persisted and brought to the late 1970s and early 1980s some of the highest inflation and interest rates that had occurred in anyone's memory (the consumer price index [CPI] exceeded 14 percent in March 1980, and the prime lending rate peaked at 20.5 percent between July and September 1981).[3]

While these late-twentieth-century economic fluctuations had huge financial implications and repercussions on America, they specifically precipitated a profound change in the life insurance industry. When interest rates were stable and predictable, life insurance thrived. Whole Life policy premiums were guaranteed. Mutual life insurers sold participating Whole Life (often referred to as "par" Whole Life), charging slightly more than the guarantee would require, but in turn paying dividends (literally a return of excess premiums) to enhance a policy's long-term benefits. By contrast, privately owned and publicly traded insurers sold non-participating ("non-par") Whole Life policies with lower guaranteed premiums but without the dividends; excess profits went to the shareholders. Whether "par" or "non-par," it was the insurance companies that assumed the investment and mortality risk inherent in the long-term promise to pay a death benefit. This was in exchange for the stipulated premium, which was reserved with a guaranteed rate of 3 or 4 percent depending on when the policy was purchased.

But when interest rates in the economy suddenly spiked to more than five times those 3–4 percent long-term rates on cash value policies, massive amounts of cash value were borrowed (or policies were surrendered) to chase the much higher returns available in money market accounts. As participating Whole Life began to suffer from the issue of such interest rate differentials, it was particularly hard on non-par Whole Life policies because there was no mechanism to pass through the insurer's higher earning potential on new fixed return investments. New sales plunged on this type of fixed "investment" life insurance, and the industry quickly introduced an entirely new form of life insurance: flexible premium Universal Life and Current Assumption Whole Life. A rapidly increasing number of older policies were surrendered on behalf of the new form of life insurance.

Flexible premium policies were first sold in 1979 and introduced the concept of uncoupling the integrally entwined financial components of premium, cash value, and expense and insurance charges within a life insurance policy. This groundbreaking departure meant, among other things, that there was no longer a fixed premium for which the insurance company guaranteed the sufficiency of the policy. Universal Life policies (the term for "flexible premium") allow policy owners to pay pretty much any amount they choose into the policy—as often or as infrequently as they wish. What is *not* obvious about such policies is that it is entirely the policy owner's responsibility to make sure that the money paid into the policy (still referred to as a "premium") plus interest credited to the account value cumulatively exceeds the policy expenses and insurance charges (see Figure 1.1 &1.2). Thus, where insurance is classically defined as policy owners shifting intolerable financial risk from themselves to an insurance company in exchange for a tolerable and predictable premium, Universal Life has an unquantifiable amount of risk that is shifted *back* to the policy owner, who often has no understanding of the magnitude of the transfer *or its cost.*

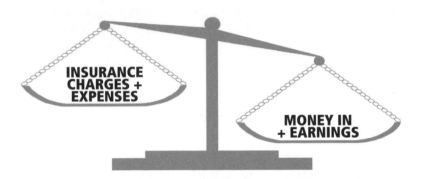

Figure 1.1   To sustain a Universal Life or Variable Universal Life policy, money paid in + interest must outweigh expenses.

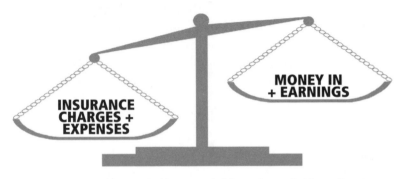

Figure 1.2   A Universal Life or Variable Universal Life policy that is out of balance will lapse—often long before life expectancy

Plentiful Policy Offerings

Our parents had a narrow choice of product offerings when it came to buying life insurance: term insurance for temporary needs and Whole Life for insurance needs that would persist as long as they lived. Technology and economic changes have allowed or encouraged the development of a much broader spectrum of policy types available to those who need life insurance. Today's sophisticated choices include Universal Life, Variable Universal Life, Variable Whole Life, Secondary Guarantee Universal Life, Equity Indexed Life, and Adjustable Life. And not only are such policies available to insure an individual, but they can also cover two or more qualified insureds. Chapter 5 includes an expanded explanation of these major policy types.

It's a Mad, Mad, Mad, Mad World

The life insurance industry got its start in the United States with the formation in 1759 of the "Corporation for Relief of Poor and Distressed Presbyterian Ministers and of the Poor and Distressed Widows and Children of Presbyterian Ministers." Later known as Covenant Life Insurance Company, it is the oldest life insurance company in continued existence (now absorbed into Nationwide Financial) in the world.[4]

The two primary forms of business organizations selling life insurance are stock companies (owned privately or publicly by individuals or institutions) and mutual companies (owned beneficially by their policyholders). As a general rule, older (100 years or more) and larger insurers tend to be mutual; newer companies tend to be stock. By 1988, the sheer number of life insurance companies in the United States peaked at 2,343, with just 118 mutual insurance companies and 2,225 stock insurance companies. While clearly outnumbered in these statistics, 6 of the top 10 insurers ranked by assets in 1988 were mutual carriers and accounted for 70 percent of the assets of the top 10.[5] Indeed, many of the traditionally trained life insurance agents today began their careers with mutual life insurers, and were often taught that "mutual was the way God intended life insurance." For many years, companies selling participating life insurance policies (where policyholders participate in profits of the insurer that are not otherwise needed to run the operation or bolster financial reserves) could point with great pride to the fact that their dividend scales increased over the years and delivered substantial value to policyholders who continued to maintain those policies. But a new wisdom has presumed itself on the industry today, namely, the notion that the only way for an insurance company to survive among highly competitive financial services peers is to have access to outside capital and become part of the food chain, wherein some will eat and others will be eaten. With the first demutualizations occurring only since the inflation/interest spike of the late 1970s and early '80s, there is not yet much evidence to suggest which business organization format will continue to deliver the most value. At the same time, however, there is an expectation that an insurance company run for and on behalf of its policyholders is likely to make decisions that are more focused on its policy owners than those insurers whose first obligation is to their shareholders.

Of those 6 large mutual insurers dominating the top 10 list by assets in 1988, only New York Life and Northwestern Mutual retain their mutual status; the rest have demutualized and, in some cases, merged with other insurers. Note that while TIAA-CREF - a "top 10" insurer in both 1988 and 2004 - is not technically mutual, it is operated for the benefit of its policyholders.[6]

Life Insurance in 2005

The consumer's dictionary of terms is different today than it was 25 years ago. "Mutual" is a term infrequently heard; "life settlements" and their cousin "viaticals" are becoming both popular and controversial. The word "premium" has new meaning—for both agents and consumers. "Risk shifting" is just as likely to mean a shift *to* the policy owner as a shift *away.* So that this book can be useful to the financial advisor or consumer, following are a few key terms and their definitions that will clarify meaning and allow easier reading. There are additional definitions in the glossary found on page 149.

- *Term* life insurance: Policies sold for a specific duration. Premiums are generally guaranteed for that duration and then are subject to market pricing (notwithstanding high guarantees) to renew beyond the original period of time.

- *Permanent* life insurance: Policies sold for lifetime needs. Policies may have specified premiums, wherein the insurer guarantees the sufficiency of the policy, or indeterminate premiums, which require policy owners to manage the economics and the risk of maintaining the policy throughout the insured's lifetime.

- *Level* premium: Generally refers to the initial period of a term policy in which the premiums are both guaranteed and constant. At the end of the initial period, premiums will generally increase annually and at a significantly higher rate than the level premium.

- *Indeterminate* premium: A specific characteristic of Universal and Variable Universal policies in which the premium is estimated but not guaranteed. It is the policy owner's responsibility to manage policy payments to ensure the sufficiency of the policy.

- *Funding* premium: The appropriate term to describe premiums for policies that are designed without fixed premiums. By adopting the modifier "funding," policyholders won't fall into the understandable trap of believing that the premium quoted for Universal Life conveys the same assurance it won't change as that of its Whole Life cousin.

- *Cash value*: The reserve created in *permanent* life insurance from the premium overpayment in early years of the amount the insurer needs to cover its death benefit liability. This reserve is important in later years when the annual cost of the liability is significantly greater than the premium. The cash value is an asset of the policy's owner. Indeterminate premium policies lapsed in the first 10–15 years may have a surrender charge, reducing the net cash value.

- *Surrender value:* The value for which any policy with cash value can be surrendered. In a participating Whole Life policy, the surrender value is typically equal to the cash value. The surrender value may be less in indeterminate premium policies, depending on how long the policy was in force before surrender.

- *Account value*: Especially applicable to Variable Universal Life and Universal Life, the account value is equivalent to the policy's cash value before the deduction of any applicable surrender charges when determining the policy's net *surrender value.*

- *Net amount at risk*: The difference between the gross death benefit and the cash value. The net amount at risk should be largest in the early years, and progressively diminish as the insured gets older, corresponding to the smaller risk of dying in a given year when young and the higher risk of death in a given year as one gets older.

- *Gross return*: Generally a term for Variable Universal Life, a gross return is the long-term average return assumed to be earned before deducting the management fees and other expenses described in the prospectus. Variable Universal Life illustrations almost always assume a gross return, not to exceed the regulatory maximum of 12 percent. Annual fees can range from 0.25 percent to more than 2.0 percent of the account value.

- *Net return*: Insurers selling and managing Universal Life and Current Assumption Whole Life policies will declare, from time to time, a policy cash value interest crediting rate subject to the guaranteed minimum specified in the policy. Both the declared and the minimum crediting rates are *net* of investment management expenses.

Twenty-First Century Life Insurance Statistics

Fifty years ago, Whole Life insurance was a staple in the small array of policies available to protect one's family or business from economic loss at the time of death. As America's economy became more complex, and as technology and economic necessity encouraged evolutionary product offerings, amounts of life insurance—and the types of policies purchased—have transformed.

Slightly less than $50 billion of life insurance was purchased in 1955; $1.6 trillion was purchased in 2003 (the last year for which industry data is available).[7] That year, Current Assumption and Indeterminate premium policies out-sold Whole Life almost 2 to 1 based on premium as a percentage of market share. Permanent insurance (again by premium as a percentage of market share) out-sold term more than 3 to 1:

Table 1.1

Policy Type	Premium as % of Market Share
Term	22%
Whole Life	27%
Universal Life	35%
Variable Life	15%
Variable Whole Life	1%[8]

Chapter 2

Why Do People
Buy Life Insurance?

The classic circumstance of the ideal insurable risk is when the potential loss has extreme financial consequences but the probability of such loss is *low*. The economic model is that an insurance company can collect a relatively small premium from the many who have similar risk profiles, earn a reasonable profit, and have sufficient reserves to cover the liability should it occur. Seemingly contrary to that model, life insurance is a contractual arrangement in which the policy owner makes periodic payments to a life insurance company on behalf of an insured so that there will be a substantial income tax-free cash amount paid at the insured's death, no matter how soon that might happen, *and even though—but for timing—the event is a certainty*. What makes life insurance work, then, is that in large groups (one million or more) of individuals, there is a high degree of *certainty* on how many of those one million will die each year. During times of plagues, wars, peace, and terrorist attacks such as 9/11, the likelihood is fairly constant that in a group of a million 37-year-old males, one thousand will die this year.[1]

No one can say *when* a specific individual will die. Thus, insurance companies can create a viable economic model to insure certainties, as long as the distribution of risk is determinable.

Because we don't know when someone healthy enough to qualify will die, the timeframes are likely to span many decades, making life insurance a financial intangible. Furthermore, life insurance is not typically thought of as something one would touch or "enjoy" during the life of the insured. When purchased in large amounts, the premiums paid can be substantial without a current benefit other than peace of mind. So with almost $1.6 trillion "individual" (as opposed to group, credit, etc.) life insurance policies purchased in 2000[2], why do people *buy* so much life insurance? Of course there are many reasons, but at a practical level it boils down to this: We buy life insurance either because we *love* someone or because we *owe* someone.

Income Replacement

Devoted readers of Agatha Christie novels—or viewers of the *Matlock* television series—know that the human body contains roughly $9.80 worth of chemicals and useful minerals. At the other end of the financial scale, *human life value* is a calculation of what we're worth as economic beings, and it takes into account our education, talents, and income earning potential. The calculation of human life value is most usually made in wrongful death lawsuits where a family is arguing for indemnification of the loss of the breadwinner's current and future earnings. For individuals in their 30s earning $100,000, the human life value can easily be projected in the $3–$5 million range when inflation and natural increases in salary are projected through a normal life expectancy. Ultimately, it is this capital sum that is deployed to replace the individual's earning capacity.

In the world of life insurance, *income replacement* is the practical manifestation of human life value, and is probably at the top of most people's list of reasons why they buy life insurance. It is almost always acquired out of love. Whether consisting of one earner or two, most households in the United States cannot survive for long without the wage earner's income(s). After all, it's not as if we just put all our earnings aside for a rainy day. There are mortgages and car payments and medical bills and food and entertainment, not to mention insurance premiums for health, fire, flood, and disability. Given that most households are lucky if there's *anything* left over at the end of the month, consider the financial impact of the premature death of a wage earner on whom the family's survival is dependent.

It's fairly straightforward to estimate the financial loss: If death removes $5,000 a month of gross earnings and there is no other source of income to pick up the slack for ongoing expenses, insurance would ideally replace most of the $5,000 *and* make sure that there are appropriate increases in the future to compensate for rising costs because of inflation and new needs as children get older. Certainly there will be some adjustments to the $5,000: We won't have to worry about Social Security or other employment taxes, but there may also be some increased expenses without a second pair of hands around the house.

Unfortunately, translating this simple calculation into a capital sum (and ultimately to a life insurance need) becomes a little more complicated and somewhat daunting. If we make *simplistic* assumptions about the future—for example, the need for $5,000 a month growing at 3 percent each year for a spouse who's likely to live another 60 years—the capital sum needed to provide that stream of income (assuming 4 percent returns) is almost $2.7 million with no principal remaining at the end of that period of time. With an intermediate step establishing debits and credits for existing assets and immediate expenses at death, this is the process typically brought to the calculation of "how much life insurance do I need?"

The problem is that most of us can't *imagine* ever seeing $2.4 million, much less buying that much life insurance to replace $5,000 a month. As a result, most people do *not* insure any more than a fraction of their *human life value*, perhaps compromising by purchasing a $250,000 term life insurance policy for a situation needing $5,000 per month. Yet such a policy would cover a family's expenses for less than four years.

Estate Liquidity

There can be significant and immediate costs associated with death, including final expenses, debts, business continuity needs, and, of course, transfer expenses and income *and* estate taxes. The gradual repeal of the federal estate tax begun in 2001 has given hope to many that life insurance would no longer be needed for that purpose, but the currently scheduled *reappearance* of the estate tax in 2011 gives pause for concern and calls on the second reason people buy life insurance: because they *owe* someone. With the current level of federal deficits, it would appear that outright and permanent repeal is less likely, but it is also probable that Congress will provide for *some* estate tax relief. The most often suggested form of relief is to increase the minimum taxable estate to between $3 and $5 million. If this occurs, there will still be a need for estate liquidity for estates over this threshold, and life insurance is one of the easiest and least expensive ways of making sure the needed funds are in the right place at the right time. When set up and managed appropriately, life insurance proceeds can be free not only of income tax (a key benefit of life insurance) but of estate taxes as well.

Estate Creation

Life insurance can help pay for estate taxes and costs on estates large enough to warrant them, but most estates are too small for estate taxes. Unfortunately, such estates may also be too small to provide for families in the way the testator might prefer. In other words, some people feel strongly about creating an estate the "old fashioned way," allowing someone to inherit it. Because of life insurance's unique income tax-free status and the ability to establish ownership to avoid inclusion in an estate that would otherwise not incur an estate tax, life insurance is an ideal way to create an estate at death. Options include the use of an Irrevocable Life Insurance Trust (ILIT) or direct ownership by the intended beneficiary with premiums paid with annual gifts.

Supplemental Retirement Withdrawals

While cash value is a necessary component of any permanent life insurance policy, participating Whole Life, Universal Life, and Variable Universal Life policies lend themselves to *overfunding* of premiums for the purpose of generating more cash value than the policy needs to sustain itself. That accomplished, it's possible to withdraw and/or borrow cash values from an existing policy to help supplement retirement income; under current tax law, cash value loans are not subject to income tax. There is one important caution: The policy must remain in force until death or a substantial amount of what has been taken out of the policy may be subject to current income (not capital gains) taxes. Those interested in such a design should consult with a professional life insurance agent to make certain they are allocating appropriate premiums at the time the policy is acquired.

Special Needs

Another typical use for life insurance (and another homage to buying life insurance out of love) is to manage the special needs of certain beneficiaries. With baby boomers also considered the "sandwich" generation, they are at the same time both parents of *children* who will not be able to provide for themselves and children of *parents* who are not able to fully provide for themselves. These and other similar circumstances lend themselves to the use of customized trusts funded by life insurance. Because of the human element inherent in this type of use, care should be taken in selecting a trustee. In the case of those beneficiaries for whom there may be a long life expectancy, it may be necessary to select a corporate trustee as a "primary" fiduciary along with an individual who well knows and cares about the particular circumstances.

Charitable Considerations

Americans gave almost $250 billion to charity in 2002.[3] In addition to annual donations and testamentary bequests, a growing amount of such largess is coming directly from the proceeds of life insurance on the lives of benefactors. A policy can be purchased and owned and paid for by the insured, with the charity as the named beneficiary (typically allowing for an estate exclusion of the amount of the proceeds), or a policy can be donated directly to a charity (typically allowing for an income tax deduction for the cash value of the policy at the time of the gift). In the latter example, the benefactor may continue to make cash gifts to the charity to support the policy premiums, or the policy may have been "paid up" at the inception of the transfer. Life insurance provides leverage between the annual premium and the ultimate death benefit. Therefore, regardless of the mechanics of transfer, life insurance purchased for charitable purposes is, for many, the only opportunity to make a significant capital contribution (perhaps resulting in a named building or facility) without the outright transfer of the capital itself.

Transforming Needs

So far we've covered the personal use of life insurance for income replacement, estate liquidity, estate creation, special needs, and charitable giving. Interestingly, not all of the needs in this diverse list necessarily exist at one time. It's possible to imagine, for example, a couple with two high-paying professional occupations facing a well-defined budgetary crisis if one were to die prematurely—but, at the same time, having no particular problems with estate taxes, special needs, or motivation to bequeath a wing to the local hospital. Assuming neither dies young, and their careers mature, retirement will become a planning focus. At some point, assets will begin taking over the job of providing the lifestyle to which they had wanted to become accustomed. The replacement of earned income is no longer a concern, but estate preservation, liquidity, access to cash values, special needs, and charitable concerns may now, to one extent or another, become part of financial planning in their maturity. The death benefit of a large term policy purchased to handle the contingency of premature death will now be needed for other long-term purposes, but the policy may become unaffordable (or unconvertible) to continue for any practical period. Transforming needs should ideally be anticipated—at least in concept—at the time of policy selection, and more will be said about this topic in Chapter 7.

Business Needs

Businesses need life insurance because businesses depend on individuals who may die prematurely. Whether it's a partnership of individuals seeking to avoid finding themselves in business with a deceased partner's spouse, a bank whose conditions for lending include adequate life insurance, or indemnification in the event of the loss of a key person, business uses for life insurance are considerable. While there have been some well-publicized esoteric plans of life insurance to offset retirement benefit costs covering many workers (so-called "janitor" insurance), these are a small portion of the total. Business-oriented life insurance is an extremely important part of almost every business continuation plan. Policies can be owned by the business in support of an "entity" stock purchase plan (easier to pay for, especially if participating insureds have significantly different premiums, but with no corresponding increase in the tax basis of shares owned by the survivors). Policies also can be cross-owned by partners or shareholders—with no involvement of the business entity itself—to facilitate the acquisition of shares at the death of a partner or owner (leaving each partner to bear the policy expense of the other partner(s), but also resulting in increased tax basis for surviving shareholders). In all cases, life insurance for business continuity should be the financial supplement for a written business continuation agreement. Additionally, life insurance maintained on the lives of key employees can offset banking and line-of-credit restrictions placed on small businesses when a principal dies.

Additional Considerations in Owning Life Insurance

Life insurance is personal property, and the policy must be titled in the name of the insured or another person or entity with an insurable interest in the individual. When the insured is the owner of the policy, the insured may designate anyone he or she wishes as beneficiary and, unless he or she has previously placed a restriction on changes, the owner is free to change the beneficiary designation whenever he or she wants. Often there is a desire to have someone *else* own a life insurance policy, including trusts, for the purpose of avoiding estate taxes on the death benefit. When the insured is *not* the owner of the policy, the owner and the beneficiary must be *identical* to avoid adverse gift taxes (gifts in contemplation of death) at the time of death.

As previously noted, life insurance proceeds received by a beneficiary generally are deemed to be free of income tax, but unless the policy is outside of the policy owner's estate, the death benefit generally will be included in the policy owner's estate for purposes of determining any estate tax liability.

Chapter 3

How Much Do I Need?

Financial advisors and life insurance agents typically will help a client understand and quantify the loss of income or estate value whenever death might occur. While typically this will lead to answering the question "how much life insurance do I need," ideally we would keep our focus on quantifying the *need* long enough to decide whether that loss or shortfall is tolerable or intolerable. An estate owner with $10 million of taxable value might be facing shrinkage of one-third to one-half of that estate because of taxes and liquidity costs; a family may be facing the loss of $5,000 per month of gross income if the wage earner dies before retirement. Yet the key questions to be asked are these: *Is this important to you? Do you care?* While the answer may seem obvious as to the loss of monthly earning power, it is by no means a given that everyone cares. Thus, we seek to distinguish between the quantification of the loss and the translation of that potential loss to the need for life insurance to offset some or all of that loss. Taking this additional step in the process serves to solidify the need *and its translation to the purchase of life insurance*, if that's the appropriate step for a given individual or business.

Once it is confirmed that life insurance is an appropriate solution, life insurance proceeds to replace lost opportunity is a simple concept: In exchange for premiums budgeted and paid over a lifetime (however short or long it proves to be), cash resources are delivered by the insurance company to the designated beneficiary at the time they are needed the most. The proceeds might provide for a surviving family's ongoing lifestyle needs, equalize legacies to those family members who are not participants in a family-owned business, facilitate a business partnership agreement for buyout at death, or provide an endowment to the decedent's alma matter. There are many more potential uses for life insurance, but common in their consideration is the following question: How much do we need?

Income Replacement

The brief example in Chapter 2 of a $5,000 monthly budget shortfall suggests a procedure for transforming current living requirements into a lump sum capitalization of the amount required to meet long-term survivors' needs. Additional considerations include the following:

- Other resources, including investments, bank accounts, and group or other life insurance benefits can be *subtracted* from the tentative capitalization.

- Certain resources—such as Individual Retirement Accounts (IRAs), 401(k) accounts, and home equity—should *not* be subtracted, because they have other intended purposes.

- Other income resources—such as the surviving spouse's anticipated income—can offset the capitalization only if the "need" wasn't based on considerations above and beyond current resources. Social Security will provide a benefit for children under the age of 16 and should be taken into account.

- The need to reduce or eliminate debt (including the possibility of eliminating the home mortgage); provide for college educations; and provide for any special needs of children, surviving spouse, or elderly parents should be taken into account.

- The need to increase future payments for the expectation of inflation should be calculated.

- Duration of need is an important component. Many couples will consider having the surviving spouse *not* work until minor children have gone to college. In this case, consideration should be given to the likelihood of a return to remunerative work, and the likely duration of such earnings.

- The retirement income needs of the surviving spouse should be estimated because the loss of a portion of the family wage income also suggests the loss of accumulating retirement funds.

Figure 3.1 demonstrates the financial categories a needs analysis might include.

Figure 3.1

Financial Needs in the Event of Death Questionnaire

Do you believe you have any of the following financial needs in the event of premature death? Please check those that apply AND indicate the longest period of time (counting from today) you believe the need may exist:

Paying for Ongoing Family Expenses When a Wage Earner Dies Prematurely:

❑ Spouse #1

Provide $_____ per month to my family for _____ years independent of any other assets or income that may be available.

Should this amount rise each year with inflation?   Y   N

This need will expire in _____ years.

❑ Spouse #2

Provide $_____ per month to my family for _____ years independent of any other assets or income that may be available.

Should this amount rise each year with inflation?   Y   N

This need will expire in _____ years.

Paying for College Expenses When a Wage Earner Dies Prematurely:

❑ Spouse #1

Provide funding for college education independent of any other assets or income that may be available:

Child 1 $ _____ per year for _____ years beginning in 20_____

Child 2 $ _____ per year for _____ years beginning in 20_____

Child 3 $ _____ per year for _____ years beginning in 20_____

Child 4 $ _____ per year for _____ years beginning in 20_____

❑ Spouse #2

Provide funding for college education independent of any other assets or income that may be available:

Child 1 $ _____ per year for _____ years beginning in 20_____

Child 2 $ _____ per year for _____ years beginning in 20_____

Child 3 $ _____ per year for _____ years beginning in 20_____

Child 4 $ _____ per year for _____ years beginning in 20_____

Reducing or Eliminating Debt (Including Home Mortgage) When a Wage Earner Dies Prematurely:

❑ Spouse #1

Pay off $_____ long-term debt (including home mortgage). This need exists for _____ years.

❑ Spouse #2

Pay off $_____ long-term debt (including home mortgage). This need exists for _____ years.

If I Survive the Need for Income Replacement, College Education, and Debt Reduction:

❑ Spouse #1

Assuming I survive income replacement, college education, and/or debt reduction needs, consider structuring life insurance policies to provide supplemental income BACK to me in the amount of $ _____ per month beginning at age _____ for _____ years.

❑ Spouse #2

Assuming I survive income replacement, college education, and/or debt reduction needs, consider structuring life insurance policies to provide supplemental income BACK to me in the amount of $ _____ per month beginning at age _____ for _____ years.

Regardless of When I Die, Estate Taxes and Costs May Exceed Liquidity – or – I Want to Leave a Specified Amount to My Heirs Net of Those Taxes and Costs:

❑ Spouse #1

Provide at least $_____ at the time of my death to leave cash for the payment of taxes and other expenses.

❑ Spouse #2

Provide at least $_____ at the time of my death to leave cash for the payment of taxes and other expenses.

Estate Liquidity

When life insurance satisfies the "owe someone" purpose of buying a policy, the *amount* of insurance is generally both objective and obvious. The determination of amount may also seem objective in the closely related estate liquidity situation ("owing" federal and state taxes and the other immediate costs of death), except there are still important subjective considerations. Life insurance does not *eliminate* the taxes, expenses, and shrinkage of value caused by liquidity crunches; it simply provides the cash to mitigate the problem. If concerned about estate shrinkage because of taxes, most financial planners would first look at the projected value of the estate after shrinkage and ask the following question: "Is this enough for your heirs?" Thus, acquiring life insurance based on a shortfall in the intended net legacy is probably a better initial approach than funding the taxes and expenses themselves.

Another issue surrounding the amount of insurance for estate liquidity is that of timing and valuation. When estimating estate costs, is the estimate based on the expectation of death *this* year, 10 years from now, or at the assumed life expectancy? Many assumptions need to be made in the attempt to accurately project values, and the longer the duration, the less likely the accuracy. Some advisors will suggest acquiring more insurance than might be immediately necessary, because age, health, and lifestyle dramatically affect the cost and availability of life insurance. Thus, determining the amount of life insurance for estate liquidity (or net legacies) remains a highly subjective process.

Business Life Insurance

As previously discussed, life insurance purchased in the context of business needs typically indemnifies the business (or its partners or owners) for economic loss at the time of death. A buy-sell agreement will specify a set amount or a formula for valuing a partner's or shareholder's interest, and life insurance ensures the funding of the business's, partner's, or shareholder's obligation to acquire the business interest from the estate of the decedent. If the agreement includes a stipulated amount, the "how much" life insurance issue should be fairly straightforward. If the agreement is based on a formula, however, there will once again be the need to anticipate growth in the valuation of the business to ensure adequate, future buyout resources. Buy-sell agreements should be reviewed frequently, as should the underlying life insurance policies to ensure that everyone's expectations will be met.

Key person life insurance often requires a sophisticated approach to the "how much" question. Certainly, the death of a chief executive officer will have a harsher economic impact on the company and its shareholders or partners than the loss of a bookkeeper. However, if that bookkeeper's unique ability, longevity, and expertise is key to providing a current stream of accurate and credible accounting data, the "valuation" picture might change significantly. The question of whom to insure and for how much would generally *first* be based on a calculation of the expected financial loss to the business from that individual's death, irrespective of potential insurance proceeds. Issues to be considered include the following:

- Cost to find a replacement
- Loss in "market" valuation, whether the business is privately or publicly held
- "Calling" of business loans or lines of credit
- Loss of current or future business opportunities
- Loss of irreplaceable management skill

Once defined, the next step is to determine whether that loss is potentially so significant that it should be *insured*. The distinction here is that the quantified liability exists whether or not it is insured. Life insurance should be considered if the magnitude of death and its financial consequence is so great that it would imperil the survival of the business or have an unacceptable effect on the financial statements of the business.

Balancing Needs

It's not uncommon in family businesses for one or more adult children to *not* be involved in that business. Testamentary provisions, trusts, and/or business buy-sell agreements may be used to effectively transfer the business to active family members at the death of the founders, but it may be inappropriate to equally transfer business interests to the uninvolved family members. Life insurance can be an excellent way to equalize the value of the legacies to the uninvolved family members, the calculation of which should be fairly straightforward.

Chapter 4

A Short Tutorial on the Mathematics of Life Insurance

You are 37 and concerned that if you die prematurely, your family will be struggling to pay its bills. If life insurance didn't exist, what would you do to make sure that, in spite of the low odds of death at such a young age, you could mitigate the financial disaster that death would cause?

You might start with a group of 1,000 of your closest and dearest friends who are in the same age group and predicament. You could make a binding, lifetime agreement that the group will collect sufficient money from each member at the beginning of the year so that on learning of any member's death, $1 million will be paid out of the group's accumulated funds on behalf of the grieving spouse, regardless of when death occurs.

Fortunately, one of the members has a degree in actuarial science and is able to determine that there's little more than a 0.1 percent likelihood of a death in the first year, suggesting that each member's contribution in the first year is just $1,000 to cover the anticipated death.[1]

Of course, it's critical that there are sufficient funds to make such payments, not just in the first year, but in subsequent years as the group gets older, with special attention being paid to what happens to the group members. You ask the actuary to look ahead a bit and give you an idea of how this lifetime agreement might affect your budget in, say, 20 years. While the odds of deaths are still pretty low for the group of now 57 year olds, the group itself is a little smaller for the 67 deaths that have occurred since the agreement began. So the twentieth-year contribution needs to be the result of that year's potential number of deaths divided by the remaining number in the group—that is, seven deaths divided by 933 (times $1 million), for an expected contribution of $7,503.

Looking even further ahead, you discover that 43 years from the inception of this plan, half of the original group of 1,000 are expected to have died. At that point, you will have contributed a total of $702,823 to provide benefits to spouses, and in that 43rd year the anticipated 36 deaths means you will need to contribute $73,620 (see Figure 4.1).

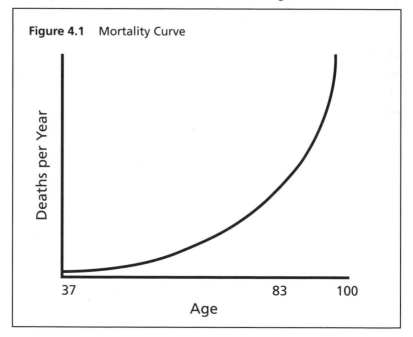

Figure 4.1   Mortality Curve

What was once a modest $1,000 annual contribution for a large payment to an unfortunate spouse is now so enormous that you would have to risk personal bankruptcy to make the current year's payment. If it weren't for the legal and moral bond you made so many years ago, you wouldn't consider making the current payment unless you knew your family was likely to be one of this year's beneficiaries.

The good news is that there really are insurance companies and life insurance policies to alleviate the administrative burden of what has just been described. But the bad news is that the cost to "pass the hat" in this hypothetical alternative to life insurance is indicative of how much life insurance will cost in any given year—and that the only way to guess what your cumulative life insurance cost will be is to begin with life expectancy calculations. However, unlike the previous example, survivors don't have an obligation to continue paying premiums to an insurance company, which introduces a significant disadvantage to the company: at some point, only the unhealthy will continue their term premiums! This "adverse selection" is taken into account in policy pricing, and term premiums beyond age 65 or 70 are substantially higher than the pure mortality cost would otherwise suggest.

On the basis of current life expectancies, a 37-year old has an equal chance of surviving or dying by age 80. From 37 to age 80, he or she will pay approximately $750,000 for annually renewable term insurance (the closest analogue to annual probabilities of death). This amounts to 75

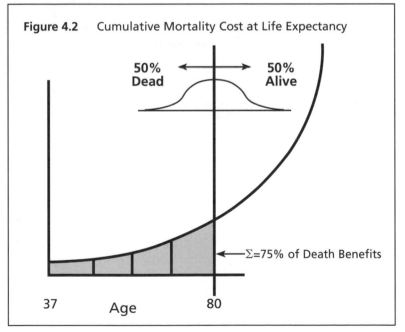

Figure 4.2   Cumulative Mortality Cost at Life Expectancy

Figures 4.2 through 4.6 are adapted with permission from copyrighted material of BTA Advisory Group.

percent of the ultimate death benefit. If the 37-year old manages to live to one standard deviation beyond his age group's life expectancy (age 90) and continues to pay the premium, the cumulative cost for life insurance will be 190 percent of the ultimate death benefit. Two standards of deviation (age 96) suggests a cumulative cost of 330 percent of the ultimate death benefit (see Figure 4.2).

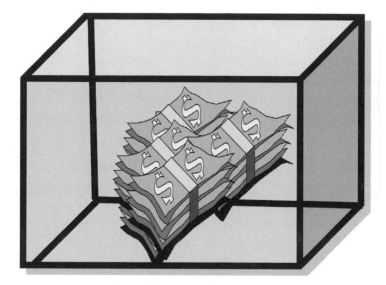

Figure 4.3   To better manage the long-term mortality costs, actuaries determined that if you put this much money in The Box™, it will pay all of the mortality costs during your entire life.

If you need life insurance for more than a relatively short period of time, you probably won't want to play the odds so far described. Rather, you're going to want to put your contributions into some kind of investment box that—depending only on administrative expenses and how much you can earn on your money—will make certain that your mortality expenses are always covered, regardless of when death occurs (see Figure 4.3).

This raises some interesting funding possibilities. While most of us would prefer to put a predictable, level amount of money into the account each year, others might want to pay it all in one lump sum or pay it in over a relatively short period of time (see Figure 4.4).

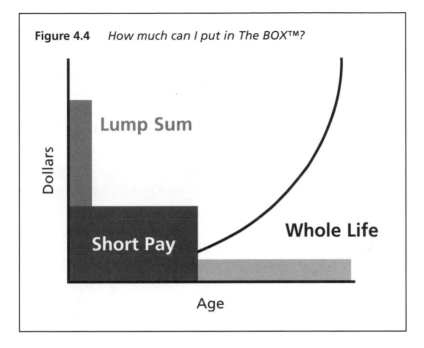

Figure 4.4 *How much can I put in The BOX™?*

Dollars

Lump Sum

Short Pay

Whole Life

Age

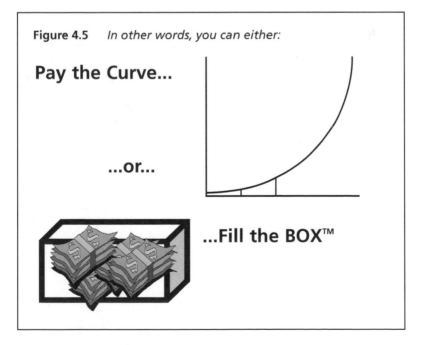

Figure 4.5 *In other words, you can either:*

Pay the Curve...

...or...

...Fill the BOX™

Whether paid in one lump or paid over time, what you pay will be a function of the present value of future anticipated mortality charges, accounting for an estimate of how much interest will be earned on your money. Higher returns suggest lower contributions; lower returns suggest higher contributions.

Short-Term Versus Long-Term Insurance

When the need for insurance is of short duration—typically 15 years or less—it makes sense to "pay the curve." However, when the need for life insurance is long, indeterminate, or lifetime, it makes sense to approach the program by filling "the box," because paying the curve will become disastrously expensive (see Figure 4.5). Filling the box is better known as permanent or cash value life insurance and, more specifically, is implemented through Whole Life and the newer Universal and Variable Universal Life policies that enable premium management and also shift the risk of financial management to the policy owner (see Figure 4.6).

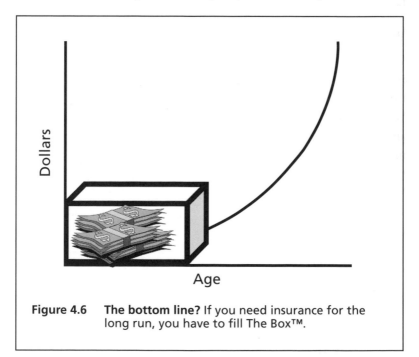

Figure 4.6   The bottom line? If you need insurance for the long run, you have to fill The Box™.

Chapter 5

Policies with Premiums

A major distinction that should be made with today's high-tech policies is whether there is a specific, *guaranteed* premium. Guaranteed premium offerings include Whole Life, the initial duration of term insurance, Current Assumption Whole Life, and No Lapse/Secondary Guarantee Universal Life.

Whole Life Policies

Whole Life is the granddaddy of all forms of long-term life insurance. It is both the most complicated and the least flexible—yet at the same time perhaps the most simple—life insurance policy developed to date. Whole Life stipulates a lifetime premium that must be paid when billed and, in return, provides a guarantee that the policy will be in force no matter when the insured dies (subject only to the financial viability of the insurer). Whole Life integrates all the mathematical elements of life insurance: premium, cash value, investment returns, expenses, and mortality charges. There is no transparency of expense elements as with newer policy forms. Whole Life is often portrayed as permanent or cash value life insurance, even though there are other forms of life insurance that suggest both permanence and contain elements of cash value.

As seen in Figure 5.1, the payment of a fixed and stipulated premium will provide lifetime coverage with a guaranteed annual increase in cash value. Every element of the policy is guaranteed except, in the case of a participating policy, the refund of a portion of the premium called a dividend. Dividends can be taken in cash, can reduce the currently due

Figure 5.1 Whole Life Insurance

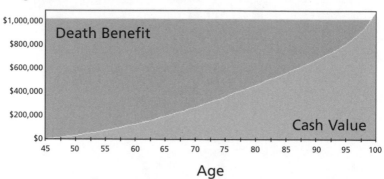

premium, or can purchase additional permanent amounts of life insurance. But until paid, dividends are *not* guaranteed.

Perhaps the least understood aspect of Whole Life—and indeed of permanent life insurance in general—is the purpose of the policy element called *cash value*. Cash value is created by the payment of a level premium that, in the early years, is significantly higher than the underlying cost of the yearly risk of death. These excess premiums accumulate each

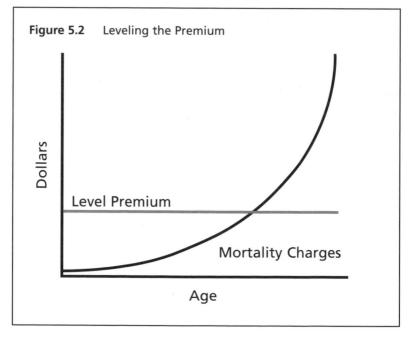

Figure 5.2 Leveling the Premium

year and essentially earn the insurance carrier's contractually guaranteed rate of return, building a reserve for risk charges that will be substantially higher than the level premium in the insured's later years (see Figure 5.2, which is in essence The Box™ described in Chapter 4). The death benefit of a Whole Life policy consists of the cash value and what the insurance company calls its *net amount at risk*. The net amount at risk is always the exposed portion of the death benefit that exceeds the cash value. As the graphs in Figure 5.3 demonstrate, Whole Life policies consist of guar-

Figure 5.3   Total Death Benefit

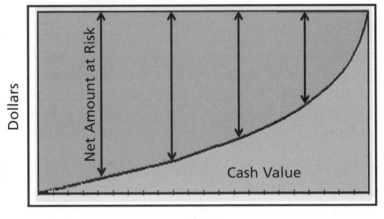

anteed amounts of gradually increasing cash value and correspondingly decreasing net amount at risk. And this would seem to be the most natural way to balance today's low probability of death with the certainty of death in the future: As the chance of death increases from year to year, the pure insurance element (the net amount at risk) decreases to manage the overall cost of the policy and allows the insurance company to guarantee the level premium. In its most elegant simplicity, the level premium defines the mathematical leveling of the mortality curve. The cash value curve of a nonparticipating Whole Life policy (see Figure 5.1) also defines the *sufficient cash value* curve that will be discussed in later chapters.

Whole Life best fulfills the need for lifetime insurance coverage for policy owners who most desire a predictable premium and, over the years, the opportunity to access a significant asset value via policy loan.

Variable Whole Life Policies

As will be described in Chapter 6, "Policies Without Premiums," there is a class of life insurance policies for which the policy owner makes all the premium investment decisions. Several life insurance companies sell a Whole Life hybrid of such policies in which there is a stipulated premium and for which certain guarantees of sufficiency will exist as long as that premium is paid.

Variable Whole Life policies provide certain guarantees for the payment of a significant annual premium, which in turn is directed into investment-oriented subaccounts. Premiums may be suspended, but guarantees will be forfeited. Insurance buyers interested in investment-oriented policies may find greater flexibility in a Variable Universal Life policy.

Survivorship Whole Life Policies

Most forms of permanent life insurance are now available in single and survivorship formats. While the Survivorship Whole Life policies sold predominantly in the 1980s had complicated and sometimes even convoluted features to achieve a "second-to-die" death benefit, today's Survivor Whole Life policies are fairly straightforward; premiums are payable until the second death, and the death benefit is payable *only* at the second death. All other features of Whole Life apply to its second-to-die cousin.

Second-to-die policies are almost exclusively used to fund estate taxes and other liabilities that occur when the second of two spouses dies with appropriate testamentary and trust provisions. While these policies enjoy more favorable pricing because of the fact that death benefits aren't paid until the second death, they should *not* be used when there will be liquidity needs for a surviving spouse. Second-to-die policies can also be used in business situations where the death of one partner or principal can be endured, but not both.

Term Life Policies

If Whole Life is the granddaddy of permanent life insurance, there is almost twice as much term life (including group life insurance) currently

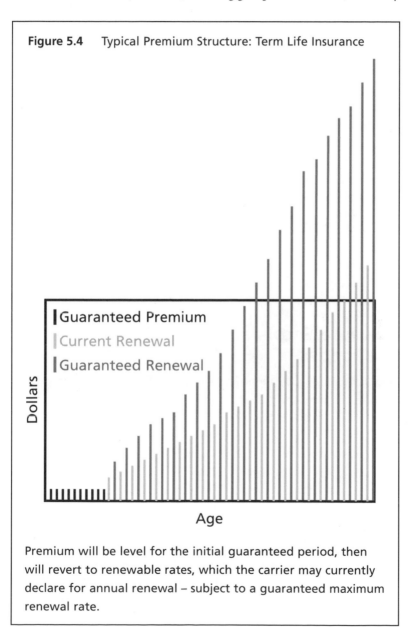

Figure 5.4 Typical Premium Structure: Term Life Insurance

Guaranteed Premium

Current Renewal

Guaranteed Renewal

Dollars

Age

Premium will be level for the initial guaranteed period, then will revert to renewable rates, which the carrier may currently declare for annual renewal – subject to a guaranteed maximum renewal rate.

providing death benefit than all other forms of life insurance.[1] Term refers to a term of years, and today's term policies are generally available for 1-, 5-, 10-, 15-, 20-, 25-, and 30-year periods. For each specified duration, the premium will typically be level and guaranteed.

There are two timeframes incorporated into this type of term policy: the guaranteed period and the period beyond the guarantee. During the guaranteed period, the level premium essentially reflects a temporary and "box"-like leveling of the mortality curve. When the guarantee period is over, premiums resume the inexorable annual increases implicit in a mortality curve. Most policies will quote *probable* renewal premiums beyond the guarantee with a substantially higher guaranteed maximum for each attained age. The insurance company has complete discretion over what it can charge for the renewal premium, subject only to the scheduled maximum (see Figure 5.4).

Because term premiums are directly related to the increasing probability of death as an individual ages, term policies are best suited for short-term or specified-term needs. However, because of the extremely long joint life expectancies and the adverse selection inherent in term life insurance, few if any insurers offer second-to-die term policies.

No Lapse/Secondary Guarantee Universal Life Policies

Traditional Universal Life policies—which will be described in greater detail in the next chapter—have unscheduled and unspecified premiums. The policy owner is responsible for making certain that cumulative payments—plus changeable policy interest credits—will be sufficient to maintain and balance the cash value and net amount at risk elements. If a policy's cash value doesn't follow the mathematic model (gradual increases, in turn causing decreases in net amount at risk), the policy will lapse when the cash value falls to $0. This could easily occur before the life expectancy of the insured. A No Lapse/Secondary Guarantee Universal Life policy, however, will *waive* the requirement to maintain positive cash value and will sustain the policy until the death of the insured *in spite of the fact there is no cash value.* At least one requirement of a typical Secondary Guarantee policy is that the specified premium must be paid immediately upon billing.

On the face of it, such a policy design mimics the most important element of a Whole Life policy: a level and fixed premium. However, because the requirement to maintain cash value has been waived, the policy is perhaps better defined as "level premium term life insurance until death." In such policies, it's unlikely that meaningful cash values will accrue beyond the 10th or 15th year (see Figure 5.5).

Figure 5.5   No-Lapse/Secondary Guarantee UL

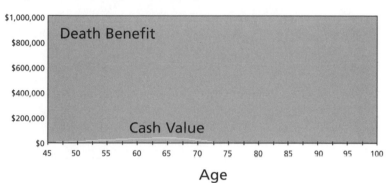

Section 3 further discusses the best uses for Secondary Guarantee policies, but their dominant benefit is a fixed and guaranteed premium that is substantially lower than that of a Whole Life policy. Families with budget constraints but long-term or life-long insurance needs might find the Secondary Guarantee policy a good premium compromise between term and Whole Life policies.

Survivorship Secondary Guarantee Universal Life Policies

As with other survivorship policies, Survivorship Secondary Guarantee Universal Life functions similarly to its single insured cousin.

Chapter 6

Policies without Premiums

As discussed in Chapter 5, a key distinction among today's life insurance policies is whether or not there is a specific, *guaranteed* premium. Offerings of policies *without* specified premiums include Universal Life, Variable Universal Life, Adjustable Life, and Equity Indexed Life.

Universal Life Policies

As previously described, Universal Life is a flexible premium policy that largely shifts the responsibility for policy *sufficiency* to the policy owner. When a premium is paid, there are distinct debits for policy expenses (including premium loads, premium taxes, and other charges), and credits for interest as declared by the insurance company. As long as the result leaves a positive balance in the cash value account, the policy is considered "in force" until the next monthly reconciliation of premium, cash value, expenses, and credits. A Universal Life policy will provide for a minimum interest crediting rate (today's new policies may guarantee only 2 ½–3 percent) and a schedule of maximum insurance charges. When economic or market conditions allow, policies may receive an interest crediting rate that is higher than guaranteed, and may be charged a lower insurance expense than is scheduled in the policy.

One valuable feature of Universal Life policies is the *transparency* of expense charges and interest credits. All elements of the policy's monthly administration are distinct and generally accounted for in an annual policyholder statement. Another term of art for Universal Life policies is "current assumption," suggesting that policy illustrations portray long-term results based on assumptions that are more favorable than those guaranteed in the policy. Current illustration regulations require that policy values illustrated under the current assumptions of the insurer also be recalculated to reflect a guarantees-only projection as well as a midpoint projection for the stipulated funding premium. Note, however, that the alternative projections will be based on the premium calculated by the *current* projection or a premium otherwise chosen by the agent. An alternative projection (using reduced assumptions) rarely recalculates a sufficient funding premium with those reduced assumptions (see Figures 6.1 & 6.2).

Figure 6.1 Traditional UL – Illustrated Results (Current Experience)

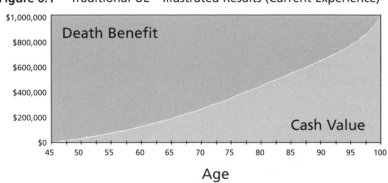

Figure 6.2 Traditional UL – Potential Risk (Reduced Assumptions)

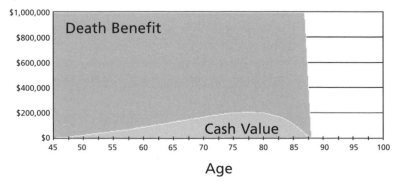

Universal Life policies are best used for policybuyers who are balancing the need for lifetime insurance and the desire to manage their premium flow. For example, unlike Whole Life, policy owners could minimally fund their Universal Life policy during the family formation/lower-income years, begin to put in more money as increasing income allows, eliminate premiums entirely while paying for college educations, and then resume with robust premium funding during the higher-earning years preceding retirement.

Survivorship Universal Life Policies

Survivorship Universal Life insures the lives of two individuals—almost always husband and wife—and pays a death benefit at the latter of the two deaths, as long as the policy is in force when the second death occurs. Early policies maintained separate mortality expectations for each spouse, but most Survivorship Universal Life policies today blend the mortality expectation into one table of insurance charges. All things being equal, the second death life expectancy of a healthy couple is longer than the life expectancy of either individual.

Variable Universal Life Policies

Variable Universal Life is a variation on Universal Life that requires the policy owner to invest the premiums into one or more of the offered sub-accounts, which are very similar to mutual fund accounts. Typically the offerings include a number of fixed return accounts, bond accounts, and equity accounts, including small cap, large cap, and international funds. Unless accompanied by a high premium requirement, there are no investment account guarantees, but there will always be a schedule of maximum insurance charges in the policy. As with Universal Life, Variable Universal Life policies are typically illustrated on a current assumption basis, with policy values projected using a stipulated premium payment under guaranteed insurance charges/zero percent average return and a current assumption of current insurance charges and a client-selected, average investment rate of return projection not to exceed 12 percent (see Figure 6.3 & 6.4).

Figure 6.3 Traditional VUL – Illustrated Results (Average rate of return)

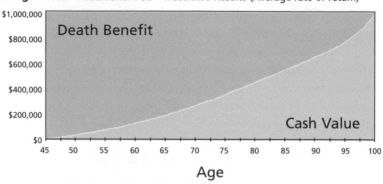

Figure 6.4 Traditional VUL – Potential Risk (Volatile Returns)

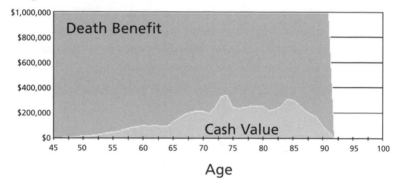

Survivorship Variable Universal Life Policies

Survivorship Variable Universal Life covers two lives and pays a death benefit on the latter death. As with the one-life Variable Universal Life, the policy owner allocates the premium into subaccounts. All other aspects of Survivorship Variable Universal Life pertain to Survivorship Universal Life.

Less Common Policy Forms

Equity Indexed Universal Life Policies

As equity market volatility began to become a fact of life in the 1990s, several life insurers developed a Universal Life hybrid. This new policy, called Equity Indexed Universal Life, has a crediting rate associated with equity indexes of the broad markets plus mechanisms to moderate losses when equities are otherwise falling. Such policies are suitable for clients who don't have risk tolerance for the volatility of a pure equity Variable Univeral Life policy, but also don't want to miss some of the "play" of rising equities in general. In other words, these clients would like to have their proverbial cake and eat it too, and Equity Indexed Universal Life policies appear to accommodate that desire quite nicely. (For the solvency sensitive, however, note while **Variable Universal Life** policy cash values are considered segregated from the general assets of the insurer and not subject to the claims of creditors, Equity Indexed Universal Life policy cash values are typically in the General Account of the insurer and thus subject to the claims of creditors should the company have financial difficulty.) While it would seem that such policies should have become more popular, their features and constructs are sophisticated and take more time and training than many insurance agents are willing to invest. Survivorship versions are also sold.

Adjustable Life Policies

As Universal Life policies became popular in the early 1980s (with as much as a 40 percent market share of new, permanent life sales), several life insurance companies produced yet another variation on flexible premium policies with the introduction of so-called Adjustable Life policies. Policy owners choose the initial premium and protection combination that fits their current needs, with flexibility to shift the policy's emphasis from protection to accumulation by increasing or decreasing either the insurance amount or the premium that goes to accumulation.

As is the case with WL policies, in-force illustrations for Adjustable Life policies are more difficult to evaluate with external tools, so care must be taken with the issuing life insurance company to request illustration variations that reflect more conservative assumptions than those that currently drive the in-force calculations.

In the next section, we'll consider how to best fund a policy that doesn't have premiums.

Chapter 7

What Kind of Policy Best Meets My Needs?

As suggested in Chapter 3, the *amount* of the potential economic loss at the death of a loved one or a valuable employee is a key consideration in determining whether an individual or business will self-insure that potential loss—or whether the magnitude is simply too great *not* to offset that liability with life insurance. When attempting to suggest the most appropriate type of life insurance policy for a specific situation and need, the first consideration is how long that need or needs exist.

While it can be a little tricky understanding the pricing of so-called "permanent" life insurance policies, nothing could be simpler than term life insurance. When matched to a short-term need for coverage, the most popular term life policies are ideal and come in five-year increments, from 5 to 30 years. Situations, obligations, or needs with a significant risk of financial loss because of death in the short run could include the following:

- Loans or mortgages of fixed duration

- Fixed-term alimony obligations

- Business buy-sell agreements within a well-defined duration

- A 55-year-old worker's earning power in the remaining 10 years to retirement

In each of those instances—notwithstanding the possibility of transforming needs (as discussed in Chapter 2)—a term policy with level, guaranteed premiums and a duration set for the far end of the needed time frame will most often be the most appropriate and economic solution to insuring intolerable risks. But underestimating the duration (or choosing shorter duration policies because of their lower cost) is a specific hazard with term life insurance. As explained in Chapter 5, term policies are relatively inexpensive for their guaranteed duration because of the statistical likelihood the insured will survive that period, but premiums beyond the initial guarantee period will rapidly escalate.

At the opposite end of the duration range, situations, obligations, or needs with a significant risk of financial loss because of death in the long run could include the following:

- The earning power of a 30-year-old entrepreneur

- Long-term debts or mortgages

- Business continuity agreements for established family enterprises

- Estate transfer costs

- Estate creation

- Estate equalization

In each of these long-term financial indemnity examples, responding to the "what kind" question is the trickier task. Whether for term or permanent, the mathematics of premium calculations suggest that the level annual premium charged by the insurer derives from the present value of the probabilities of death in each of the years being insured. Because that probability rises each year that we live, longer durations have a higher cumulative probability, and therefore higher premiums. Remember that the cumulative mortality costs to life expectancy reach a significant percentage of the death benefit itself. There are substantially lower ultimate mortality charges in permanent policies since the adverse selection inherent in term insurance is not present.

As a general rule, the crossover for the decision between level premium term and level premium permanent life insurance is approximately 15–20 years. Needs that are indeterminable—or lifetime—will almost always point to some form of permanent life insurance.

Thus, the debate between "term or perm" can be reasonably resolved based on the duration of need, subject to budgetary considerations. But while there are only two types of term life insurance (annually renewable and fixed duration), there is a much broader spectrum of permanent life insurance policies with sometimes subtle differences in opportunities and risks. It is here that the broader financial planning model of modern portfolio theory, asset classes, and asset allocation is useful. Consider that permanent life insurance comes in variations that range from fully guaranteed to fully risk-based. Pricing issues should be secondary; the questions each policy owner needs to consider are these:

- What is your life insurance policy *style?*

- With what types of risks are you comfortable or uncomfortable?

- How much exposure to risk can you tolerate?

- Are you as comfortable taking risk in your life insurance policy cash values as you are in your general investment portfolio?

Readers will find a questionnaire in Appendix 1 designed to suggest an insurance buyer's risk tolerance and insurance style. The scoring works as follows:

> **Scores ranging from 6–15** suggest a *conservative* approach to investing. Preserving principal is most important, with an average annual total return typically ranging from 2 to 5 percent. Adjusted for inflation, investment returns may be very low or, in some years, negative. This is the tradeoff for very high liquidity and essentially no risk of principal loss. People in this risk category typically choose Whole Life policies to meet their long-term life insurance needs

(typically 15 or more years) and guaranteed premium term insurance for the full duration of their lengthiest purpose for life insurance (typically less than 15 years).

Scores ranging from 16–25 suggest a *conservative-to-moderate* approach to investing. Preserving principal and generating some income is most important, with an average annual total return typically ranging from 5 to 7 percent. This investor's willingness to accept some risk is inferred from seeking a modest, positive, real (after-inflation) rate of return. People in this risk category typically choose Whole Life or Universal Life policies to meet their long-term life insurance needs (typically 15 or more years) and guaranteed premium term insurance for the full duration of their lengthiest purpose for life insurance (typically less than 15 years).

Scores ranging from 26–34 suggest a *moderate* approach to investing and a willingness to trade possible principal loss in pursuit of higher total return, typically ranging from 7 to 9 percent. Risk can be reduced through diversification, holding periods, asset allocation, and periodic rebalancing any excesses that develop. People in this risk category typically choose Variable Universal Life (VUL) policies with a balanced allocation, to meet their long-term life insurance needs (typically 15 or more years) and guaranteed premium term insurance for the full duration of their lengthiest purpose for life insurance (typically less than 15 years).

Scores ranging from 35–44 suggest a *moderate-to-aggressive* approach to investing. This score suggests a willingness to accept risk of price volatility to achieve growth. The average annual return typically ranges from 8 to 10 percent. More active portfolio adjustment to the portfolio is a typical feature of this type of investor's behavior. People in this risk category typically choose Variable Universal Life policies, with an aggressive allocation, to meet their long-term life insurance needs (typically 15 or more years) and guaranteed premium term insurance for the full duration of their lengthiest purpose for life insurance (typically less than 15 years).

Scores ranging from 45–54 suggest an *aggressive* approach to investing. This investor is willing to take substantial risk in seeking to achieve above-average growth over time. The typical average annual total return in this category is considered to be 10 percent or greater. More concentrated positions and frequent portfolio changes typify this type of investor. Investors in this category may experience a wide variance in results from one year to the next in pursuit of long-term goals. Investors in this category are assumed to be experienced and sophisticated with such investments, and typically have a long timeframe in which to achieve their goals. People in this risk category typically choose VUL policies, with a very aggressive allocation, to meet their long-term life insurance needs (typically 15 or more years) and guaranteed premium term insurance for the full duration of their lengthiest purpose for life insurance (typically less than 15 years).

Chapter 8

From Which Company Should I Buy a Life Insurance Policy?

I n our parents' day, Oldsmobiles were pitched as putting a "rocket in your pocket," and life insurance companies were as solid as ... well, the Rock of Gibraltar. Name-brand carriers were respected and never failed. A.M. Best was the sole rating agency assessing the financial health of America's insurers, and most of the top 100 (out of a field of more than 2,000) received the highest rating of A+.

But the 10 year period from the late 1970s to the late 1980s that provoked such dramatic changes in product offerings also created significant financial instability in an industry that depended to a substantial degree on level interest rates. In April 1991, Executive Life (13th largest U.S. insurer) was seized by California's Insurance Commissioner and liquidated. Several months later, Mutual Benefit (a top 10 U.S. insurer) was seized by New Jersey's Insurance Commissioner and also liquidated. In 1992 , The Equitable Life Assurance Company (the third largest U.S. insurer) agreed to demutualize and be acquired by the French insurer AXA rather than suffer a financial collapse.[1] The fallout would continue through the decade with the last major insolvency occurring at Missouri's General American Life, which acquiesced in 1999 to voluntary rehabilitation and a merger with MetLife.

Today's life insurance companies have transformed both themselves and their products in an attempt to protect against a repeat of the last decade's financial dissonance. Universal Life and Variable Universal Life policies shift the premium sufficiency risk to the policy owner; such policies represented roughly 50 percent of new sales in 2003.[2] Whole Life and No Lapse/Secondary Guarantee Universal Life are backed by the carrier's financial stability. Term (during its initial guarantee period) is also backed by the carrier's financial stability, but sufficiency risk is shifted to the policy owner during the period beyond the initial guarantee in which death is more likely to occur.

While there are still unique product offerings that may be offered by some companies, the selection of an insurance company should follow standards of prudence and due diligence in an economic environment characterized by volatility and instability. The following standards for choosing a life insurance company are recommended:

- Choose carriers with financial ratings from at least three of the major ratings services (e.g., A.M. Best, Moody's, Standard & Poor's, Fitch, and Weiss).

- Choose carriers that have financial ratings of at least A+ from A. M. Best and that are not less than fifth from the top rating categories of the other agencies (e.g., Moody's, A1 or better; Standard & Poor's and Fitch, A+ or better; Weiss, B or better). There is rarely a compelling reason to make exceptions.

- Recognize that, while cheap term is often offered by small insurance companies, the cost difference is minor to acquire term from a larger company.

- If buying term, consider policies offering conversion features that can solve the emerging problem of lessening insurability and longer time frames than initially expected when the term policy is first acquired.

- Choose a carrier offering policy types and *features* that are attractive to you and that seem to fulfill your needs.

- Do *not* choose a carrier based on its policy illustrations, appearance of competitive pricing, or other nonguaranteed representations.

- If buying permanent life insurance, consider whether your *insurance style* suggests more comfort with a mutual insurer or a stock insurer.

There's an old saying among life insurance agents: Life insurance is *sold*, it's not *bought*. There's probably a good deal of truth in that; we aren't inclined to consider unpleasant possibilities, and for most of us, that includes the prospect of dying. A skilled life insurance agent or broker does not necessarily have all the answers you might need, but he or she *must* have all the questions! The consideration of which life insurance company to buy from is simply a logical end of the process that started with the following: Do I need life insurance? If so, how much? With an amount in mind, what kind of policy will best meet my needs, circumstances, and risk tolerance?

Section 2

Logical Decisions, Illogical Results: *Why Do Bad Things Happen to Good Policies?*

Chapter 9

The Walmart Paradigm: Low Prices—Always!

Wh ile Sam Walton might not have been the first to discern that you can "get the business" if you beat the competition at pricing commodities the customer wants, he certainly succeeded in embedding this marketing concept in the psyche of the American consumer. Service, features, and benefits can also be important in the purchasing decision, but once those are determined, *price* is the ultimate determinant influencing where (or with whom) we will conduct our business. Low pricing is why Walmart is the number one retailer, with more employees and more revenue than any other retail business establishment in the world.

This buying paradigm, having captivated the minds and hearts of retail buyers, has found a new home among prospective life insurance owners. "I want a $1 million policy; tell me your *price* and I'll compare it with five other proposals and let you know which I'm going to buy." In the trade, this is called "spreadsheeting." While this approach can be effective at pricing commodities bought and used without subjective considerations such as comfort, durability, or aesthetics (gasoline, paperclips, and paper towels come to mind), it is *impossible* to quantify the potential cost of one flexible premium Universal Life or Variable Universal Life policy versus another. There are simply too many moving parts that can be repriced by the insurance company as, over time, it gains experience with its in-force policies. At first glance, these products defy the concept of simplicity. Let's review the nature of these pricing elements.

Mortality Expense

There is less than a 0.2 percent chance that a healthy 45-year-old woman will die *this* year. Her statistical life expectancy suggests that she has an *equal chance* of dying before or living beyond age 84. Her 75-year-old mother has more than 14 times her daughter's chance that death could occur *this* year, but for having survived to age 75, she has a statistical life expectancy of age 88. These statistics are drawn from *mortality tables* that account for the probability of deaths within a very large statistical sample (typically a group of 1 million).[1] Most of us have no idea when we'll die; only a fictional actuary with the last name of Soprano is likely to give us the time, place, and method of our demise!

Mortality expense, therefore, is a fundamental element of the expenses to be met by a life insurance company as it sells policies to millions of individuals and for which death claims will be paid out over many years. At the outset, an insurer's mortality expense is an estimate based on current experience, yet its future experience *will change.* This estimate is translated into its Cost of Insurance (COI) element in Current Assumption policies.

Interest or Investment Income

Life insurance companies maintain policy reserves in their General Account to be able to at all times cover their liabilities—principally death and living benefits associated with policies they have sold. These assets consist of a significant percentage (typically 80–90 percent or more) of high grade bonds and mortgages, plus a relatively small portfolio of equities, and myriad other incidental investments. Income from its investment portfolio will be the principal driver of the investment component of dividends or the interest crediting rate on UL, non-par Whole Life (WL), or Adjustable Life policies. The portfolio rate of return will vary with the level of safe returns available in the current economy. General Account policies include Whole Life, Universal Life, No Lapse Universal Life, Adjustable Life, and term.

Expenses

An insurance company's expenses—other than mortality expenses—include rent, utilities, wages, taxes, and sales commissions, to name just a few. An insurance company that can manage its expenses will have an edge in producing profits for its policyholders (mutual insurers) or increased revenue per share for its shareholders. It's also important for an insurance company to sell a significant number of policies to help drive down its unit expenses; the more policies, the more that fixed expenses can be spread against the total, and the lower those costs will be for individual policies.

Lapses

In the last 20 years, assumptions about how long policyholders will voluntarily keep their policies (if not resulting in a death claim) have become a pricing consideration in developing new policies and illustrations. To the extent that an insurance company prices its policies for early profit *and* policyholders quit their policies in the early years, it is possible to assume those gains into later-year illustrated policy benefits. Of course this is a form of tontine, and it was generally forbidden by policy illustration regulations adopted by most states in the late 1990s. Still, some form of lapse-support in the design of policies is assumed to exist.

With respect to each of these pricing elements, insurers must make assumptions based on forecasts that span 40, 50, 60, *or more* years. If you want a price guarantee, the insurance company is going to have to be either extremely prescient or extremely conservative in its calculation of these underlying pricing elements. Because attempts at reading financial crystal balls often lead to bankruptcy, life insurers will opt for the conservative approach to pricing, the result of which has been the Whole Life policy—and more recently the No Lapse/Secondary Guarantee Universal Life policy.

The Bottom Line

An important issue implied by the overuse of policy illustrations is the belief that one insurance company must be better than another if its illustrated premiums are lower or its illustrated benefits are higher. But when considering the projection of current assumptions about costs and portfolio earnings far into the future and the insurance company's ability to adjust those pricing elements, is it *credible* to assume the illustration defines who's better and who's worse? The answer is an emphatic *no!* Furthermore, as far as mortality expense is concerned, it isn't credible that *peer* companies would have dramatically different experiences over long periods of time while insuring tens of millions of people. As for long-term investment performance, peer companies (who, among other things, enjoy very similar financial ratings) are in virtual lockstep with respect to investment quality and therefore investment performance.

Most insurance company actuaries will privately acknowledge that *in spite of* dramatic differences in illustrated cost or benefits, actual long-term policy performance of *similar* policy types among *peer* carriers will be much more *similar* than those illustrations otherwise suggest.

Chapter 10

Policies and Their Illustrations

Non-Variable Life insurance policies have two basic documents that are delivered to the new policy owner: the policy and a policy illustration. (The purchase of a Variable UL or WL policy also requires delivery of a prospectus.) The policy is a legal contract; it specifies the terms and conditions under which the policy has been purchased and for which the death benefit will be paid. The policy will specify the insured, the death benefit, and the premium (stipulated or flexible). The policy illustration, however, is for the most part a finely crafted work of fiction, deploying and projecting changeable variables far into the future of assumptions that are current but not guaranteed—and taking the most critical assumption factors and using them as *constants*. Yet, like Damien and Pythias, Romeo and Juliet, and Yin and Yang, these documents are inexorably tied together by insurers and their agents—not to mention the expectations of the marketplace.

Policy illustrations, rather than being part of the policy (a legal contract), are in fact marketing documents, attempting to highlight the best aspects of the financial potential for the policy. A policy illustration is therefore no better, and no worse, than advertising materials whose purpose is to attract the potential buyer to buy this policy rather than that policy. However, since the introduction of flexible premium Universal Life policies in 1979, the illustration has taken on a practical chore that it cannot possibly or reasonably accomplish: to solve the dilemma that it's hard to sell a policy when that policy type has no premium in the traditional sense.

Thus, the illustration quickly became the tool to calculate a premium based on some inherent, constant assumptions about future expenses, policy earnings, profit margins, and mortality charges. The insurance company, however, reserves the right to increase those expenses and/or change the policy earnings expectations—in essence to reprice the policy over time, subject to the schedule of maximum charges and, in the case of Universal Life, minimum crediting rates enumerated in the policy.

This practical characterization of a life insurance policy illustration is not intended to suggest there's anything inherently wrong or bad with Universal Life/Variable Universal Life policies or their illustrations; it's simply that those dealing with these policies must understand the difference between the policy and the illustration and have a pragmatic and useful approach to manage such policies.

Indeed, the classic illustration dilemma is summarized in Table 10.1: How is it possible for there to be so many different "prices" for the same thing? The data in Table 10.1 indicates that the guaranteed premium for a nonparticipating Whole Life on a 45-year-old male in good health is $15,255 for a $1 million policy. As long as this premium is paid each year—as required under the policy/contract—the $1 million death benefit will be paid to the designated beneficiary no matter when death occurs. Were it issued by a mutual carrier, the premium might be slightly higher (a representative premium for a dividend-paying policy is $18,810); the higher premium is justified by a historic ability to enhance policy values and benefits through the payment of dividends (or to offer cash refunds that allow for a lower net policy premium). To keep it simple, we'll use the non-par Whole Life premium of $15,255 as our benchmark for a fully sufficient, guaranteed premium paid on behalf of a $1 million policy. With equal guarantees of sufficiency, a representative No Lapse/Secondary Guarantee Universal Life premium is $8,041; the difference between these two guaranteed policies is the strong likelihood that the latter will develop no accessible cash surrender value beyond the 15th year of ownership.

Then there's the calculation of "premiums" for those policy types that *have* no premiums. Using current assumptions of a 5 percent crediting rate and the currently assumed scale of future Cost of Insurance, a regular Universal Life calculation of funding premium is $10,400. A Variable Universal Life policy—assuming 10 percent average long-term investment returns in all-equity subaccounts—could be funded for as little as $7,178.

Table 10.1 Summary of Classic Illustration Dilemma

Healthy 45-Male	Guaranteed Premium	Calculated Funding Premium
Non-Par Whole Life	$15,255	
Par Whole Life	$18,810	
No Lapse Universal Life	$8,041	
Universal Life		$10,400
Variable Universal Life		$7,178

One intriguing issue of computer-generated policy illustrations is that, when premiums or cash values are presented as a precise number (e.g., $7,178), the seeming accuracy of such a calculation has a subtle but powerful effect on most consumers: it's easy to automatically assume that the precisely calculated numbers are themselves *accurate!* But nothing could be further from the truth.

The Society of Financial Service Professionals attempted to help agents, insurers, and their customers break the code of arcane insurance language and the assumptions underlying the production of a policy illustration. In the Society of Financial Service Professionals' groundbreaking Illustration Questionnaire introduced in 1992, the introduction states, in part:

> ... sales illustrations are useful in developing the best combination of policy specifications to achieve the buyer's objective. However, illustrations have little value in predicting actual performance or in comparing products and companies ... sales illustrations are usually designed to present potential benefits and costs under a set of non-guaranteed assumptions more optimistic than the guarantees ... [and] the risks associated

with the possible inability of a product to achieve the higher illustrated benefits, or lower illustrated costs, than those generated by the guarantees are borne by the policyholder.[1]

The National Association of Insurance Commissioners (NAIC), in its December 1996 promulgation of Model Regulations for life insurance policy illustrations, defined the purpose of an illustration as "clearly disclosing how the policy being illustrated will work, distinguishing that which is guaranteed and that which is not." Among other objectives, the NAIC said the illustration must be "understandable to all parties involved in the sale of life insurance." In spite of four years of dedicated effort attempting to tame a freight train hurtling toward a concrete barrier at 100 miles an hour, today's regulated policy illustrations are simply incapable of accomplishing the NAIC's objectives. While it is true that regulated illustrations will contain information about guaranteed values (based on assumed funding premiums), far more questions remain than are answered. The approach to understanding how a life insurance policy really works must begin with, well, this book!

Chapter 11

Revealing (Life Insurance) Secrets of the Ages

I t defies logic that a basic commodity like life insurance can be priced so differently by so many different policy illustrations. With more than 1,500 life insurers domiciled in the United States, there certainly is no lack of open-market competitive forces. As discussed in Chapter 9 of this section, peer insurers are generally expected to incur the same broad costs and returns over the extremely long periods of time characterized by life insurance economics. And it's not as if we're describing the aesthetic and functional differences between a Yugo and a Mercedes. When it comes to pricing life insurance, there's the nonguaranteed hypothetical illustration, and there's reality.

So here's the real deal, the secret sauce, the Occam's Razor:[1]

> For any given age, gender, medical, and financial risk profile, there is a level premium that will be fully sufficient and profitable for both the contract holder and the contract issuer to provide life insurance coverage for the life of the insured, providing death benefit proceeds no matter when that life comes to an end. Any attempt to charge or pay an amount that is lower than this fully sufficient and guaranteed cost introduces a level of risk that the typical policy owner doesn't know exists and that cannot be fully quantified until after the insured has died.

Furthermore, the fully sufficient and profitable level premium herein described generates a theoretical cash value curve that will be referenced frequently in this section.

With that simple declaration of reality, we hold the following truths to be self-evident about the attempt to "get a better deal" for lifelong life insurance needs:

Truth #1
We're drawn to the attractive impossibility rather than the less attractive probability.[2]

Policy illustrations generally portray an *attractively impossible* outcome when the focus is on low price. The illustration conceals the more likely result that such an attractive price cannot possibly occur when calculated with current data projected decades into the future, when the insurer has the right to increase its internal pricing parameters, *and when the interest or investment return factors themselves are assumed to remain constant.* This truth is supported by the generic disclaimer *required* by regulators on every policy illustration: "Illustration [results] are neither a projection nor a guarantee of future results." Every sufficient level premium for every type of policy has its own *theoretical cash value* curve that must at least be matched by actual policy values for the policy to sustain for all years (see Figure 11.1).

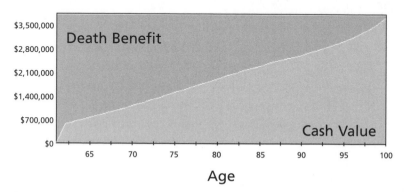

Figure 11.1   Every sufficient level premium for each type of policy has its own theoretical cash value curve that must at least be matched by actual policy value for the policy to sustain for all years.

Truth #2

Historic policy performance data is of little or no practical use in determining "which policy will perform better?"

Today's and tomorrow's economic realities are simply too different from yesterday's to encourage any significant reliance. Illustrations calculating Universal Life premiums in 1982 with 14 percent crediting rates—no matter how realistic that might have been *then*—created an unrealizable expectation as interest rates plunged to such a low level that most of the policies issued in the early 1980s are today paying only the rate guaranteed in the policy, itself a rate generally higher than otherwise warranted by current experience. Similarly, illustrations calculating Variable Universal Life premiums in 1997 with the regulated maximum illustration rate of 12 percent—no matter how realistic that might have been *then*—created an unrealizable expectation as investment returns plunged in early 2000 and left those policies with ballooning *net amounts at risk* and the very real possibility of policy lapse years before life expectancy.

Truth #3

There's a cliché that says, "If it seems too good to be true, it probably is." A second cliché says, "Promise 'em anything as long as you have the right to change it later." A third (this from a commercial ad for oil filters) says, "Pay me now or pay me later."

Life insurance companies and their agents aren't bad. Most companies are well-run businesses and most agents care about doing the right thing for their clients. But they *are* in business to sell their products. Too often a clear understanding of how things work is given inadequate attention, and it can be rationalized that it's more important for a client to buy needed coverage than to understand all the moving parts.

Truth #4

The only alternative to relying on policy illustration premium sufficiency calculations is to deploy independently derived benchmarks for each major policy type and to use stochastic (probability) analysis to introduce some reality into the otherwise unrealistic use of constant rate of return projections.

Interest rates in the U. S. economy have had significant increases and decreases in the last 40 years (see Figure 11.2). Interest rates will undoubtedly continue to undulate up and down. Similarly, investment returns have been very volatile in the last 20 years and are likely to remain so (see Figure 11.3). Because lower returns (interest or investment-based) can—all things being equal—cause *net amount at risk* to increase, the effect of this type of volatility must be taken into account. Rather than assume constancy, then, it's critical to find an economic modeling tool that will give some sense of the *likelihood* that assumptions made today will have validity for the future. Fortunately this can be done with a modeling technique popularly known as Monte Carlo Simulation, a process by which underlying returns are randomized and illustrated values recalcu-

Figure 11.2   One-Year Treasury Bills from 1966-2004

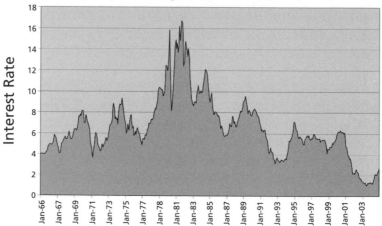

Figure 11.3   Standard & Poors 500 Rates of Return

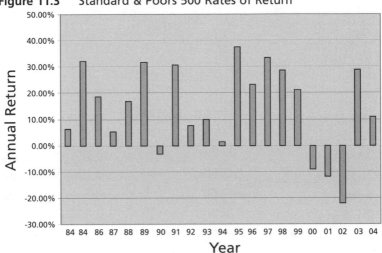

lated for a statistically credible number of cycles so that a *probability of success* can be inferred. If we were to apply this technique to the funding premiums in Table 10.1, we would see the following results:

Table 11.1   Probability policies will sustain to age 100

	Funding Premium	Calculated Probability to Sustain Policy to Age 100
Non-Par Whole Life	$15,255	100%
Par Whole Life	$18,810	100%
No Lapse Universal Life	$8,041	100%
Universal Life	$10,400	60%[3]
Variable Universal Life (all equity)	$7,178	80%[4]
Variable Universal Life (recalculated for higher probability)	$10,900	85%[5]

Figure 11.4 depicts a more visual way to appreciate an even broader spectrum of funding premium possibilities and their respective likelihood of

Figure 11.4 Various policy premiums and their respective policy types and the probability of sustaining the policy to the age of 100 for $1 million death benefit, healthy, 45-year-old male.

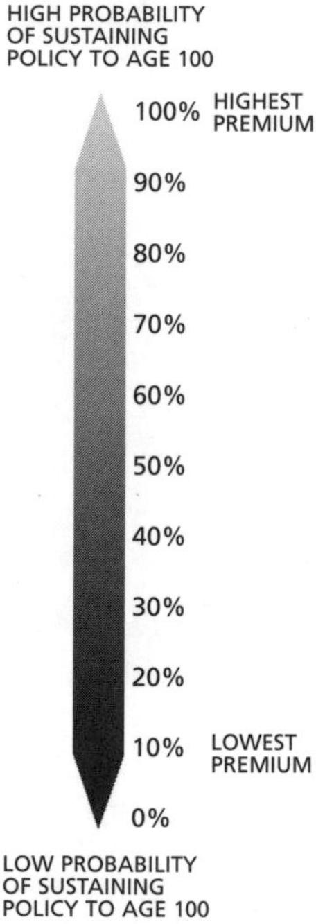

HIGH PROBABILITY
OF SUSTAINING
POLICY TO AGE 100

	Premium	Probability	Policy Type
100% HIGHEST PREMIUM			
90%	$18,800	100%	GUAR par WL
80%	$15,250	100%	GUAR non-par WL
70%	$11,500	80%	UL @ 4.35%
60%	$10,500	80%	VUL - reduced return
50%	$10,500	60%	UL @ 5%
	$9,600	40%	UL @ 5.6%
40%	$8,040	100%	No Lapse UL
30%	$7,200	80%	VUL - all equity
20%	$5,900	60%	VUL - all equity
	$5,400	40%	VUL - all equity
10% LOWEST PREMIUM			
0%			

LOW PROBABILITY
OF SUSTAINING
POLICY TO AGE 100

sustaining the policy to age 100. Is a 60 percent probability of successfully sustaining a life insurance policy to age 100 acceptable for *you*? Even those with high risk tolerances will generally require a certainty range of 80–90 percent; funding premiums accordingly must be increased, but the long-term *value* created by payment of higher funding premiums must also be taken into account, as depicted in Table 11.2.

Table 11.2 highlights a difference in policy selection that is not generally observed when looking specifically for a "low" funding premium: Anticipated ultimate death benefits can be substantially different, and perhaps lead to the final truth.

Table 11.2 Revised funding based on at least 90% probability to sustain to age 100

	Funding Premium	Calculated Probability to Sustain Policy to Age 100
Non-Par Whole Life	$15,255	100%
Par Whole Life	$18,810	100%
No Lapse Universal Life	$8,041	100%
Universal Life	$12,000	90%
Variable Universal Life (all equity)	$7,700	90%
	Projected Death Benefit Age 100	Premium/ Death Benefit I.R.R.*
Non-Par Whole Life	$1,000,000	1%
Par Whole Life	$3,500,000	3%
No Lapse Universal Life	$1,000,000	3%
Universal Life	$3,500,500	5%
Variable Universal Life (all equity)	$15,300,000	10%

*Note: Internal Rate of Return (IRR) measures the cost to its ultimate benefit. The higher the IRR, the more favorable the result.

Truth #5

There's no free lunch.

Most of us will acknowledge our attraction to a good deal; it almost seems to be human nature. But we've also purchased enough things that didn't live up to their potential as a "good deal" to suggest another truism: the *appearance* of a bargain is far more frequent than the *experience* of a bargain. There *are* things that can—and should—be pursued on the basis of best price. But current assumption / indeterminate premium life insurance isn't one of those things; as explained in this chapter, these policies need to be explored with a more sophisticated buying paradigm than just an illustrated premium portrayed and projected with the current assumptions of the insurance company.

Chapter 12

Whole Life Insurance in the Real World

100% Non-Par Whole Life
100% Par Whole Life

"In the beginning" there was Whole Life. If you're reviewing a Whole Life policy on which the full premium has been faithfully paid since it was purchased (and will continue to be paid in the future), you can skip this chapter. But since the interest rate shock of the late 1970s and early 1980s and the flexible premium policies that emerged in reaction, agents have had a more difficult time selling pure Whole Life policies. Notwithstanding the fact that a participating policy could deliver three to four times the original death benefit to the beneficiaries of an insured who lives to or beyond their life expectancy, the participating Whole Life premium (as shown in Table 11.1) can be substantially greater than the premium of a "regular" Universal Life or No Lapse Universal Life policy.

To maintain the viability of Whole Life policies for those buyers whose risk tolerance and insurance style was otherwise compatible with Whole Life policies (but who were seeking lower outlays than the typical whole life premium), in the early 1980s, insurers and agents began calculating more sophisticated ways to manage future premium payments. Insurers and agents looked at the prospect of future dividends and incorporated that expectation into the illustrated cash flow. It's critical to remember, however, that a key characteristic of a Whole Life policy is that its premium is due each and every year for the period (typically lifetime) specified in the policy. Premiums cannot be skipped; premiums cannot be "flexed." Any illustrated portrayal of premium cash flow that is less than that specified in the policy is made under a set of assumptions about future dividends that may or *may not* prove viable.

Policy Loans

Payment of the Whole Life premium is required each year until death (or the maturity of the product, such as age 95 or 100). But premium payments can come from sources other than the policy owner, and can even come from the policy itself, for example, as policy loans. At one time interest on policy loans was tax-deductible if the original payment pattern followed the "four out of seven" rule (in which four of the first seven annual premiums had to be paid in cash; only three premiums could be borrowed). But since 1986, interest on policy loans has been defined in the tax code as consumer interest, and it is therefore nondeductible, even for policies purchased before this change in the tax code. While no longer as common, occasionally an agent will show premium management techniques in policy illustrations wherein both the annual premium and the policy loan interest is borrowed from the policy. Although such payment schemes clearly illustrate an important "living" benefit of life insurance—loans cannot be "called" but are repaid at death out of policy proceeds—they're generally inadvisable as long-term premium payment solutions.

Term Blends

At the outset, Whole Life is "expensive" and term is "cheap." But if you need life insurance for a lifetime and *live* a long lifetime, Whole Life is cheap and term is expensive. In the early 1980s, a popular technique to illustrate more moderate premiums for Whole Life policies was to combine Whole Life with term blends. It was like buying two policies—a Whole Life and a term—but in this instance, the two policies were combined under one contract. Generally sold with dividend-paying Whole Life, the idea was that the dividend would be used to first pay for the term portion, and the balance of the dividend would purchase paid-up additions of life insurance. Over a period of 20 years or so, the amount of the term death benefit would be reduced in an amount equal to the increasing value of the death benefit of the paid-up additions. Under the dividend scales of those times, illustrations frequently showed a premium that was perhaps 60 percent of a traditional Whole Life premium, and whose death benefit progressively became permanent over that 20-year illustrated time span.

Blends of no more than 25 percent term have generally remained viable. But as dividend scales began declining—a reflection of lower inflation rates and therefore lower interest rates since the mid- to late-1980s—in-force illustrations for policies sold with too much blended term began to show the downside of this approach: The inevitably spiraling premium of the term portion of the policy consumes most of the lower-than-illustrated dividend and, hence, prevents the accumulation of any more paid-up additions. Total premiums begin to escalate, and unless outside funds are provided, the policy generally will start borrowing required premiums from cash value and ultimately lapse.

Premium Offset

As genuinely innovative as the creation of flexible premiums to pay for life insurance, "premium offset" anticipates the future flow of dividends and becomes an illustrated means for the policy owner to pay a certain number of the policy's lifetime required premiums out-of-pocket and then *stop* making cash payments, letting accumulated and future dividends take over the burden.

Here's how it works: The illustration's computer calculates the hypothetical number of years in which cash premiums need to be paid; let's assume it's 10 years. While the policy owner is making those premium payments, dividends are acquiring paid-up additions. Paid-up additions have both guaranteed death benefits and guaranteed cash values. The eleventh premium payment—in our example you expect to pay no more than 10—is drawn out of the cash value of the paid-up addition account. It's *not* a loan; a sufficient amount of paid-up additions cash value is simply surrendered—*tax free*. Each subsequent year that this is done, the value of the paid-up additions declines until the policy is nearly back to its original guaranteed death benefit and cash value. The computer has calculated, however, that just at the point you've exhausted the paid-up additions account, the *current* dividend is now sufficient to directly offset the premium due. Anticipating that the dividend will continue to increase, premiums are illustrated to be paid by current dividends for the balance of the insured's life, while excess dividends once again acquire paid-up additions.

Of course the only problem with this premium payment concept is that if future dividends *paid* do not match the dividend scale originally *illustrated*, this carefully calculated balancing act will be delayed and policy owners will find themselves needing to pay more yearly premiums than they expected. Unfortunately, many policy owners didn't realize the subjective nature of the illustrated expectation. As the sky-high interest rates of 20 years ago began to decline, "7 pay" schemes promoted in the mid-1980s became "20 pay" or even "30+ pay," prompting class action suits and many negotiated policy enhancement programs.

Today's policy illustrations are probably less dangerous in their *nonguaranteed* attempt to mitigate the cash flow commitment of the insurance prospect; if nothing else, today's significantly lower interest rates and dividend scales don't allow the highly speculative results that illustrations were suggesting in the 1980s. But anyone attracted to this approach to paying for life insurance must understand that, once again, the policy illustration is a marketing device and the illustration incorporating current experience in no way reflects the guarantees of the policy or the issuing life insurance company.

The description of today's Whole Life policies generally applies to par and non-par Whole Life policies, as well as to its half-brother, the Current Assumption Whole Life policy.

Chapter 13

Universal Life Insurance in the Real World: The "Flexible" and "Transparent" Policy

90% Universal Life

50% Universal Life

25% Universal Life

The introduction of Universal Life policies allowed substantially more flexibility than just that of paying a slightly lower premium. It solved many of the structurally rigid aspects of Whole Life policies, which forced tortuous (and ultimately disastrous) sales illustration schemes in the high interest rate days, and it potentially clarified how the policy actually worked through its "transparency" of itemized expenses and interest credits. Policy loans weren't necessary; term blends weren't necessary (although still used, as will be discussed); premium offset wasn't necessary. For all the seeming benefits of Universal Life policies, some wonder about the drawbacks. Well, there aren't any! Unless, that is, you don't make sufficient funding payments into this policy type to sustain it until death, and the policy lapses *before death* for lack of sufficient cash value.

Policy Mortality

To effectively use Universal Life insurance, policy owners must avoid being seduced by the appearance of an attractive premium (at least relative to a Whole Life premium) and fund the policy sufficiently. An insufficiently funded policy might "die" before the insured does. Life expectancy is determined by a year far into the future in which 50 percent of people of a certain age group (who bought life insurance) are dead, and 50 percent are still alive. Similarly, there can be a "life expectancy" for policies, calculated on the likelihood that premium funding suggested by a policy illustration will sustain the policy until the insured's anticipated death.

Table 13.1 indicates funding premiums for males, females, and joint lives as they might be calculated by a Universal Life illustration system at an assumed constant crediting rate of 5 percent (typical in 2005) and currently projected Costs of Insurance. It also indicates that the *probability of success* of such illustrated premiums—based on historic patterns of increases and decreases in interest rates—trends in the 50 percent range. This means that especially for today's 25 to 55 year olds who are likely to live to age 100, funding their Universal Life policies at the recommendation of a simplistic policy illustration has an equal chance of success *or failure* of providing the anticipated death benefit. As Table 13.1 also indicates, a modest increase in the initial funding premium can make a substantial difference in the outcome. An average, voluntary increase of 20–25 percent at younger ages and less than 5 percent at older ages produces a revised funding premium that increases the probability of success to 90 percent or greater. Because this increased funding premium is more than necessary in the early years, it enables the policy to withstand subsequent periods of lower interest rates (or modest increases in charges); the substantial increase in age 100 death benefits is the result of paying "more than you have to" (at 5%).

Term Blends

While Universal Life is itself a combination of term insurance and a side fund earning interest, term blends may still be found in new policy illustrations. The main reason such blends may be offered is to lower the potential impact of sales commissions on the economics of the policy,

Table 13.1a Healthy Males–$1 Million Universal Life Funding Premium Calculations.

Age	5% Projected Premium	Probability Sustain to 100	Average Revised Premium to 90% Probability	Resulting Age 100 Death Benefit
25	3,500	40%	6,200	8,693,000
35	5,650	40%	9,200	6,283,000
45	9,350	40%	13,650	4,703,000
55	15,400	35%	20,700	3,248,000
65	26,500	30%	32,750	2,392,000
75	46,700	10%	56,000	1,724,000

Table 13.1b Healthy Females–$1 Million Universal Life Funding Premium Calculations.

Age	5% Projected Premium	Probability Sustain to 100	Average Revised Premium to 90% Probability	Resulting Age 100 Death Benefit
25	3,000	40%	5,650	8,762,000
35	4,750	35%	8,150	5,727,000
45	7,900	40%	12,000	4,136,000
55	13,000	35%	18,000	3,057,000
65	22,100	30%	29,000	2,379,000
75	41,000	15%	50,750	1,760,000

Table 13.1c Healthy Males/Females (Joint Lives)–$1 Million Universal Life Funding Premium Calculations.

Age	5% Projected Premium	Probability Sustain to 100	Average Revised Premium to 90% Probability	Resulting Age 100 Death Benefit
45/45	5,750	60%	8,600	3,686,000
55/55	9,750	55%	13,000	2,814,000
65/65	17,250	55%	21,400	2,104,000
75/75	31,800	45%	37,000	1,599,000

because commission rates are different on the permanent portion versus the term portion.

Indeed, at least one carrier illustrates its age 45 male/preferred Universal Life with a premium of $9,217 for the generic Universal Life policy, and $7,575 for a term-blended version. In theory, the only difference in cost is the amount of the funding premium. However, when assessed with a probability analysis, it appears that the term-blended variety is more dependent on the ability of the insurance company to maintain its projection of relatively low term rates for the next 30–60 years. If the insurer is not able (or willing) to do so, the liability is the policy owner's, not the insurance company's.

Premium Financing

Premium financing for large policies (typically $5 million or more) has been introduced in the last several years and involves securing an independent source of borrowable funds to pay life insurance premiums. Special variations of Universal Life policies are used in which the death benefit can be defined as a specified amount *plus* the amount needed to repay the lender both principal and interest. Because the concept was introduced during a time in which interest rates have been historically low, there is not enough experience to suggest what could happen to such plans if interest rates spike or invert. Premium financing plans work best when the policy owner has sufficient resources to pay off the loans and resume premium payments should some external economic event otherwise begin deteriorating the plan. Premium financing should never be used for long-term or lifetime needs of life insurance in order for the policy owner to afford the policy premiums.

The Likely Direction of Interest Rates and the "Lag" Effect

In the last 25 years, the yields on 10-year Treasury bonds have ranged from 14.6 percent in early 1982 to as low as 3.75 percent in March 2003 (and still below 4% in mid-2005).[1] Shorter-term rates were even higher in the early 1980s and lower in 2003–04. Many of us who were lucky enough to have purchased a 10-year certificate of deposit (CD) in 1982 yielding 15 percent were disappointed to find that rolling over the CD in 1992 provided a much reduced yield. If you were a large life insurance company, however, you would be investing millions of dollars every day in fixed return securities with rates that varied with that day's bond market. The company's *portfolio yield* would be an average of its total income—some at higher rates for older investments, some at lower rates for newer investments. When interest rates are declining, the *portfolio yield* will be higher than new-money rates, and policy owners will enjoy the positive *lag effect* of the mathematics behind calculating *portfolio yield.* The reverse is also true: when new-money interest rates ultimately begin to increase from historic lows, there will be a negative *lag effect* on portfolios in which the average portfolio return will be lower than returns offered by new, fixed return investments.

This brief lesson in portfolio economics is important to understand the likelihood that interest crediting rates on new Universal Life policies may well *decline* for the next few years, even as new-money interest rates increase in the economy.

Universal Life policies fill an important style niche for policy owners who need more premium flexibility than allowed by Whole Life - but who are less aggressive than the style suggesting self-directed, investment-oriented policies. But Whole Life and Universal Life policies are backed by the General Account of the issuing life insurance company, and these accounts are overwhelmingly invested in high-grade, fixed-return portfolios. Dividend scales and interest crediting rates are not likely to increase for another two to five years, and this could negatively affect the expectations of buyers of such interest-sensitive policies.

This general expectation of the trend of portfolio interest rates in insurers' General Accounts will also have a large impact on in-force policies. Universal Life policies that were purchased 10 and 15 years ago were sold when crediting rates were substantially higher than they are today. In fact, crediting rates would generally be lower but for the minimum rates guaranteed by the policy. For these policies, unless interest rates rapidly return to the levels of 25 years ago (an extremely scenario), it is possible that policy crediting rates will not increase above guaranteed minimums for many years to come. Policy owners should review the described policy assessment options in Section 3.

Chapter 14

Variable Universal Life Insurance in the Real World: It's 10 PM; Do You Know Where Your Portfolio Is?

99% Variable Universal Life

50% Variable Universal Life

10% Variable Universal Life

While generally a policy for the experienced and moderate-to-agressive investor, Variable Universal Life insurance policies have grown popular as a means for policy owners to take their investment risk tolerance and desire for control, management responsibility, and opportunity into the realm of their life insurance policy. Presumably the result of a thoughtful consideration of suitability for such a product, a decision to buy a Variable Universal Life policy should be accompanied by an awareness that it is in all respects a Universal Life design but for the obligation to direct premiums and underlying cash value into sub-accounts. These sub-accounts, in turn, include the insurer's proprietary investment accounts as well as clones of offerings from the major mutual fund vendors. Sub-account offerings will typically range from aggressive (i.e. U.S. and International small-cap stocks) to conservative (i.e. U.S. Bonds and other fixed return securities), allowing the policy owner to direct an asset allocation that is appropriate for his or her risk tolerance. And, because the policy owner is taking responsibility for investing the underlying cash value, Variable Universal Life policies generally have no minimum guaranteed rate of return.

Whether on purpose or by accident, the early architects of Variable Uni-

Figure 14.1   Cash Values increase and Net Amount at Risk declines in order to sustain the policy until death.

Death Benefit

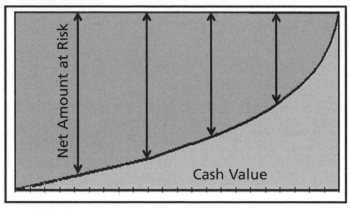

Age

versal Life took their cues from Whole Life insurance for product design and illustration systems. That is, as illustrated in Chapter 5, the death benefit of a Variable Universal Life insurance policy has two components: (1) the cash value and (2) the additional amount needed at any moment in time to equal the death benefit (see Figure 14.1).

This is both a necessary and a perfect design for Whole Life policies whose many internal working parts are guaranteed. In this discussion we'll focus on the *theoretical cash value* formed by the sustainable premium discussed in Chapter 11 and highlighted in Figure 11.1.

But when we visualize this *theoretical cash value* in Variable Universal Life insurance policies, the unthinkable can happen: the cash value can actually *decline* because of market activity or failure to maintain a sufficient funding premium to compensate for the ever-increasing risk charges. Once a variable policy's cash value declines from its theoretical and intended inexorable lifetime path (from $0 to approximately equal to the death benefit itself by the time the insured reaches age 100), the policy design requires that the net amount at risk *increase* rather than follow its plan for constant decrease. Consider, then, that the cash value of the policy is the bank account for the policy: Premiums flow into the cash value and expenses are paid from the cash value. But if cash values decline below the theoretical curve, more cash value than planned will be needed to pay for the increased net amount at risk. Visualize the policy as it is forced to ratchet up and down each month—paying more for risk charges, which reduces the cash value, which increases the net amount at risk, which increases the risk charges. If this ratcheting effect begins at age 70 or later, a Variable Universal Life policy's decline from the *theoretical cash value* and commensurately increasing net amount at risk can cre-

Figure 14.2   When Cash Value pays more for Net Amount at Risk, Cash Values fall into a negative spiral until policy lapse.

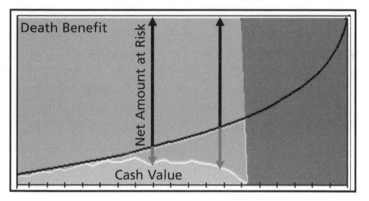

Age

ate a critical negative spiral, leading to the creation of a **swirling vortex** in which the policy is inevitably doomed to drown in as few as five years. Hence, Variable Universal Life's fundamental design can lead to a "boom or bust" result and, as will be seen, the *only* way to prevent it is to maintain a sufficient cash value at all times that can resist the inexorable ups and downs of market volatility (see Figure 14.2).

With due respect for any individual's tolerance for risk and *suitability* for such a product, Variable Universal Life represents the culmination of almost 300 years of life insurance growth and policy development in the United States. It is the perfect policy, giving its owner's discretion to manage the underlying investments in a manner that is compatible and suitable to their risk tolerance. In the spectrum of policy offerings—from conservative Whole Life through risk-tolerant Variable Universal Life—it is also the type of policy most vulnerable to the perils of using policy illustrations to evaluate the funding premium that should be paid for the policy.

All Variable Universal Life illustrations used to calculate a funding premium will render that calculation by employing a long-term average investment return assumed by the agent but not to exceed 12 percent gross of investment management fees. Today's aggressive investor might seek long-term gross average returns of 10 percent from an all-equity asset allocation, and understandably feel comfortable in using such a rate to calculate a funding premium. Tables 14.1a-f show calculated premiums for selected ages for both healthy men and healthy women, as well as a table insuring both for Survivorship Variable Universal Life. These tables depict assumptions of both all equity (meaning a relatively aggressive 100% stock allocation) and 60/40 (meaning a less aggressive allocation of 60% stocks and 40% fixed return securities) asset allocations. Variable Universal Life funding premiums range from $2,400 to almost $36,000 in an age range of 25 to 75—assuming a 10 percent long-term average rate of return—consistent with the historic returns of aggressive investors and calculated via policy illustration. But Tables 14.1a-f also highlights the problem: A 45-year-old female's calculated funding premium (all-equity allocation) of $4,200 for $1 million of coverage looks like a great bargain until we add a probability analysis and see that there's less than a 50/50 chance that her policy will sustain to and beyond age 100. This is not to suggest she definitely won't have any insurance when she dies, but it does suggest that the timing of her death may be such that she outlives her policy.

Continuing the example of the 45-year-old female seeking $1 million of lifetime coverage, we can recalculate the funding premium according to her risk tolerance and willingness to stipulate a probability of success with which she is comfortable. If 90 percent is her threshold, then her funding premium needs to be roughly $6,350, not $4,200. While this represents a dramatic 50 percent increase in annual funding for this policy, not only does she better assure herself that the policy will sustain no matter how long she lives, but the underlying statistical analysis suggests that the policy death benefit at age 100 – should she survive to that age – could exceed $14 million.

The preceding example and the accompanying tables highlight the importance of resisting the purchase of buying a Variable Universal Life policy

Table 14.1a   Healthy Males–$1 Million Variable Universal Life
Funding Premium Calculations.
100% Equity Asset Allocation

Age	10% Projected Premium	Probability Sustain to 100	Average Revised Premium to 90% Probability	Resulting Age 100 Death Benefit
25	2,400	45%	4,000	26,743,000
35	3,250	45%	4,400	15,238,000
45	5,850	60%	7,400	12,236,000
55	11,000	35%	15,500	6,667,000
65	21,400	50%	26,750	5,004,000
75	41,500	60%	46,500	3,514,000

Table 14.1b   Healthy Females–$1 Million Variable Universal Life
Funding Premium Calculations.
100% Equity Asset Allocation

Age	10% Projected Premium	Probability Sustain to 100	Average Revised Premium to 90% Probability	Resulting Age 100 Death Benefit
25	1,950	45%	3,400	27,115,000
35	2,700	45%	3,800	13,368,000
45	4,500	55%	6,050	10,019,000
55	8,400	35%	12,750	5,846,000
65	16,600	40%	22,400	4,713,000
75	32,000	35%	40,300	3,594,000

Table 14.1c   Healthy Males/Females (Joint Lives)–$1 Million Variable Universal Life Funding Premium Calculations.
100% Equity Asset Allocation

Age	10% Projected Premium	Probability Sustain to 100	Average Revised Premium to 90% Probability	Resulting Age 100 Death Benefit
45/45	1,700	55%	2,900	6,963,000
55/55	4,000	30%	8,000	4,610,000
65/65	8,100	30%	15,000	3,843,000
75/75	16,900	30%	26,250	3,002,000

Table 14.1d   Healthy Males–$1 Million Variable Universal Life Funding Premium Calculations.
60/40 Asset Allocation

Age	8% Projected Premium	Probability Sustain to 100	Average Revised Premium to 90% Probability	Resulting Age 100 Death Benefit
25	2,500	20%	4,300	7,243,000
35	4,100	40%	5,400	5,755,000
45	7,300	65%	8,400	4,936,000
55	12,700	40%	15,500	3,319,000
65	24,000	65%	27,000	3,013,000
75	45,700	75%	48,000	2,375,000

Table 14.1e   Healthy Females–$1 Million Variable Universal Life Funding Premium Calculations.
60/40 Asset Allocation

Age	8% Projected Premium	Probability Sustain to 100	Average Revised Premium to 90% Probability	Resulting Age 100 Death Benefit
25	1,950	10%	3,650	6,544,000
35	3,250	25%	4,500	4,746,000
45	5,700	55%	6,900	4,186,000
55	10,300	45%	12,800	3,039,000
65	19,200	55%	22,000	2,657,000
75	35,600	25%	41,800	2,269,000

Table 14.1f Healthy Males/Females (Joint Lives)–$1 Million Variable Universal Life Funding Premium Calculations.
60/40 Asset Allocation

Age	8% Projected Premium	Probability Sustain to 100	Average Revised Premium to 90% Probability	Resulting Age 100 Death Benefit
45/45	2,950	75%	3,600	3,085,000
55/55	5,400	45%	7,900	2,491,000
65/65	10,000	40%	14,000	2,296,000
75/75	18,900	20%	27,000	2,036,000

based on its illustrated "premium." As discussed in earlier chapters, it is the policy owner's responsibility to determine and manage the amount of the premium for a flexible premium (Universal Life or Variable Universal Life) policy under changing economic conditions. The policy owner accepts this quid pro quo when buying a policy that allows enormous flexibility in its funding. And while some agents will attempt to suggest one policy is better than another solely on the basis of which one is illustrating the lower premium, it is evident how disastrous it can be in the long run to buy a policy based on price when it had no "price" to begin with.

Key Features
When More is Less

If a funding premium is calculated to reasonably sustain the policy to age 100, the question might arise "is there any reason to pay more than that premium?" The answer is perhaps counter-intuitive: If there are sufficient

Table 14.2 Projected Cost of Insurance expenses based on different funding premiums

	COI based on Funding Premiums	
Year	$6,000	$12,000
10	$4,968	$3,198
20	$12,665	$1,332
30	$26.096	$6,071
40	$50,515	$5,295

Healthy 45-Male and $1 million coverage

Table 14.3 Projected Charges/Cash Value/Death Benefit
at Life Expectancy (age 85)

	Funding Premiums	
	$6,000	**$12,000**
Total Charges	$365,088	$140,471
Cash Value	$403,985	$3,072,383
Death Benefit	$1,000,000	$3,226,002

Healthy 45-Male and $1 million coverage

resources to pay more premium than necessary, not only does the higher funding premium give the policy a more comfortable confidence that it will sustain to age 100, but the total policy Cost of Insurance charges will be less. This is because the higher funding premium will - all things being equal - create cash value faster, thereby more quickly diminishing net amount at risk. Tables 14.2 and 14.3 demonstrate the different level of charges—and summarizes the benefits—of paying $12,000 per year for a policy that might have been "ok" at $6,000 per year.

Allocated Charges

An insurance company's monthly process for administering Variable Universal Life policies includes calculating the average net amount at risk charges for the prior month. If the resulting charges amount to $500, for example, then $500 worth of sub-account units have to be redeemed. If the value of those units has declined in the last month, more units have to be sold to produce the required "cash." If there is more than one underlying sub-account, units will be redeemed pro rata to the percentage contribution allocation. This is a form of negative "dollar cost averaging." Prospective Variable Universal Life policy owners should consider buying policies that allow a designated portion of the funding premium to go into a money market–type holding account that is then exclusively used to pay monthly risk charges. This is typically referred to as "allocated charges."

Dollar Cost Averaging

It has long been suggested that progressively investing a specific amount of money into an equity portfolio will produce the best long-term "cost per share" and therefore produce a superior profit in a portfolio. This is called dollar cost averaging. Given the concept of periodic, self-determined premiums that purchase units of sub-account value similar to that of mutual fund investment units, Variable Universal Life is an ideal candidate for dollar cost averaging and doesn't require a specific rider or policy provision; it's simply a function of how often you fund your Variable Universal Life policy.

Autorebalance

The concept of asset allocation calls for investors to create a portfolio consisting of negatively correlated investments that provide the potential for the greatest return with the lowest risk. At the highest level, the negative correlation may simply be between fixed return investments and equities. If, for example, the appropriate allocation is 60 percent equity and 40 percent fixed, a decline in the value of equities ultimately will suggest using a portion of the fixed account to acquire *more* equities at their lower price, bringing the allocation back to its original level. While investment portfolios are often professionally managed, Variable Universal Life portfolios often are *not* managed, even by the policy owner. Auto-rebalance features are available from some insurance companies and should be considered for those policy owners who don't expect to actively manage their policies.

Chapter 15

Life Settlements

Not all life insurance policies become death claims. It's estimated that fewer than 5 percent of term policies are in force at the time of the insured's death, primarily because of replacement with other policies, elimination of need, or the inexorable increase in the cost of maintaining such a policy at older ages. By definition, there's no cash value in a term policy, so when it's dropped (the policy owner indicates nonrenewal by simply not paying the premium due), that's the end of it. This was the classic wisdom until life settlements exploded into existence in 1998. A term life insurance policy about to lapse for nonrenewal could be worth as much as 25 percent of the policy's *death benefit* on the life of someone over age 70—with health issues—who no longer needs the policy. As a result of life settlements, a whole new industry has emerged, introducing "fair market value" as a term of art into policy terminology.

Because of the emerging secondary market in life insurance policies, life settlements have literally breathed new life and value into about-to-lapse and unwanted and unneeded policies. In the typical life settlement, the ideal candidate is over age 65, has experienced a deterioration of health but is not terminally ill, has a life insurance policy with a death benefit of at least $250,000, *and no longer needs or can afford the policy.*[1] The University of Pennsylvania's Wharton School estimated that in 2002, policy owners received $242 million *more* in sales proceeds than would have been forfeited to insurers if the policies had simply been dropped.[2]

The subject policy doesn't have to be term. Cash value policies also qualify (only 10 percent of issued Universal Life policies have turned into death claims in the 25 years that this policy form has existed), and Conning & Company found "…that more than 20 percent of the policies owned by seniors have life settlement values in excess of their cash surrender values."[3]

This new wrinkle in the life insurance industry poses some intriguing issues:

- If the fair market value of a policy exceeds its cash value *and the fair market value exceeds the policy owner's tax basis in the policy,* how is a sale taxed? Traditionally, when a policy is surrendered and the gross cash value exceeds the net premiums paid for the policy, the excess is taxed at ordinary income rates. Certain life settlement institutions suggest that the taxable difference between the settlement value and the cash value should be taxed at capital gain rates. Since there are currently no Treasury regulations on this issue, interested readers should seek tax counsel.

- A life insurance policy acquired on your life will become less valuable to the new owner the longer you live (and the longer that investor is paying premiums to maintain the policy). At least in theory and in the extreme, a third-party owner of a life settlement policy has an economic interest in an untimely death. As a result, life settlements are almost always purchased by institutional investment pools whose individual investors have no access to the identity of the insureds under the acquired policies.

- Life settlements provide a new option for policy owners who are concerned that they cannot afford the revised premiums required by many policies that have not met their illustrated projections. Fair market value will generally exceed the policy's cash value for those age 65+ and in less than good health.

- Financial advisors should determine an assessment of fair market value for any client over the age of 65 for whom current insurance may require a substantial increase in premium or for which the death benefit is no longer needed.

- Because insurers are concerned about the total amount of life insurance outstanding on any given individual, a new policy *may not be available.* As a result, life settlements may not be suitable as part of an exchange for a new policy.

- Key person life insurance policies on departed executives may be especially good candidates for life settlements.

- "Viaticals" are similar to life settlements, but generally focus on insureds whose physicians stipulate that the insured is terminally ill and will likely die within two years of the sale of the policy.

- Charities that have previously taken on life insurance policies from donors but now find the cash values nearly exhausted, may also be good candidates for life settlements.

Additional Details

Life settlement institutions are generally licensed by state Departments of Insurance. Investors participate in blind pools that acquire policies from individuals. Once acquired, the investment pool pays premiums for the remaining life of the policy's insured. While life settlements appear not to be subject to federal or state securities laws, some states seek to provide additional layers of consumer protection.

Section 3

What to Do With Policies That Appear to Be "Failing"

Chapter 16

To Replace (a Cash Value Policy) or Not to Replace; That Is the Question!

A Universal Life policy purchased in 1994 whose funding premium was computed at the then prevailing interest crediting rate of 6.75% is not going to be conforming to its *theoretical cash value* curve. At some point the policy owner is going to be made aware of this dilemma and will face the choice of increasing his funding premium, complaining to the insurance carrier, or exchanging into a new policy that appears to solve the problem for approximately the amount of the old policy's premium. It's estimated that 30-40% *or more* of what the life insurance industry considers "new sales" each year in fact represents the replacement of old policies with new ones. And perhaps it's understandable at a consumer consciousness level: as a corollary of the Walmart paradigm, we are well accustomed to replacing virtually every consumable we own when it no longer works. That's because in our experience it's generally cheaper to buy a new one than fix the old one. (Have you seen an appliance repair store lately? Neither have I!). We've also been convinced to replace perfectly good computers and other high tech gadgets when newer versions appear to have faster/better/niftier features. So if we discover that our life insurance isn't "working," we're conditioned to the notion that perhaps we should replace it. It's also easy to see why it seems to make sense to policy owners to upgrade the "old" one with the "new" one if an agent approaches us with a newer type of life insurance that's come on the scene.

The first important question to address: What is a "new" policy? Certainly there has been an evolution in policy types, from Whole Life through Variable Universal and Equity Indexed UL. But is a "new" policy recommendation being made primarily through its policy illustration (and therefore "numbers" orientation) or is it the result of a process that might suggest that your insurance style has changed? A second question to ask is whether this "new" VUL is better than the VUL you have now. Should you switch to a UL if you currently own a VUL? If your UL premium offset isn't working out, should you exchange to a no-lapse UL?

Life Insurance Policy Development "Life" Cycle

In spite of what has been described so far about the various types of life insurance, at a practical level there are really only two kinds of life insurance: the kind that's being suggested for you to buy and the kind that you already own. (This discussion is generally more applicable to indeterminate premium-type policies.)

Consider briefly Carrier A's product development cycle. When it addresses the development and marketing of a new policy, Carrier A is viewing the policy from the standpoint of its competitiveness and potential contribution to the bottom line. And of course competitiveness is going to be measured by the numbers shown on the policy illustration. An insurer is generally going to want those numbers to look as attractive as possible compared to their peers in the marketplace, and Carrier A's actuaries and marketing specialists look closely at their own data and experience—and that of the competition—and bring forth their finest creation to date: *Opus UL* out-illustrates every Universal Life policy currently being sold.

Of course Opus UL is a success! Trade press suggests that Carrier A's newest UL is a clear winner in the marketplace. Yet after a period of selling Opus UL to more than its share of new policyholders, other insurers in the same market space are going to catch up, improving *their* illustrated numbers accordingly. At some point, Carrier A is going to have to go back to the drawing boards. And indeed, based on new data and in anticipation of longer life expectancies, *Magnum Opus UL* is born. Carrier A stops selling Opus (technically "closing the block" of policies it has sold) and begins touting Magnum Opus in many of the same ways it introduced its predecessor. In all likelihood, agents are going to encourage the eligible Opus policyholders to make the switch to Magnum Opus. Many do, and almost everyone's happy.

However, we've just described the initial stages of *adverse selection*. Earlier in this book, readers saw an example of adverse selection in the discussion of why term insurance doesn't work at older ages—only people about to die would continue to pay term's huge renewal premiums and insurance companies would go bankrupt if their policyholders had that kind of economic control. The transition from Opus to Magnum Opus is another example of adverse selection. By drawing out the best risks from the pool of Opus UL policyholders, a less healthy group remains. The smaller, less healthy group will likely experience earlier deaths, driving up the claims experience of Carrier A and forcing it to raise its mortality charges even more. Even as those lucky enough to qualify for the newer policy enjoy *prospectively* lower mortality charges, the group remaining in Opus will likely incur higher costs.

The important question to ask: What will happen 3-5 years from now when Magnum Opus UL is in turn succeeded by *Magnum Opus ULTRA UL* in the ever spiraling competition of policy sales? It's quite likely that the much touted Magnum Opus policyholders will be split into those who can qualify to "upgrade" and those who can't. For those who can, it's important to also appreciate that successfully qualifying to go from one policy to another—chasing the illustrated appearance of best price—also has the immediate cost of surrender charges on the old policy, new sales commissions, and yet more surrender charges to be imposed if there's yet another round of replacements in the future.

The lesson learned: Every "new" policy will become an "old" policy in the same way that a showroom car becomes a used car as you depart the dealership.

Reasons to Replace Life Insurance: By the Numbers

If the recommendation or consideration to change policies is based on the "numbers," you may already be in trouble. Recall the usefulness of illustrated numbers: unless they're guaranteed, you can't rely on illustrated values whose underlying charges can be changed from those originally assumed by the insurance company.

Yet there "are" numbers that should reasonably be taken into account. If a UL or VUL policy has so badly deteriorated due to external economic forces (or simply the failure to pay funding premiums for a number of years), it indeed may make more sense to buy a new policy than to attempt to put the older policy back on its *theoretical cash value* curve. The same could hold true for a Whole Life policy that has been heavily borrowed on to pay the required premiums and dividend scales have not been sufficient to help out. Make sure to determine whether you'll have a taxable gain on surrender. Ordinary income taxes are assessed on the excess of gross cash value over net premiums paid - without regard to policy loans diminishing the surrender value.

Reasons to Replace Life Insurance: Something's Changed

Let's face it: Virtually nothing in life works out exactly as planned. For the most part, life insurance companies aren't intentionally "baiting and switching." Policies that don't work out the way we expected are the result of some combination of significant changes in our economy, market volatility, our desire to get the best deal and/or the inclination to skip a premium we don't have to pay. Change is what's most constant in our lives, and we shouldn't expect long-term financial decisions to survive without some adjustments. As life insurance policies and new associated features are developed, it certainly makes sense to determine whether a switch to a new policy provides a net gain on the basis of something other than the *numbers*. Here are issues that could compel looking at a new policy:

- Important new features that can't be added to existing policies: newly developed *living benefit* riders, including Long Term Care provisions that give the policy owner the ability to draw down on a policy's death benefit to pay for those eligible expenses.

- Your underwriting category has *improved* since you bought the first policy, but the insurance company refuses to amend your current policy to reflect such an improvement.

- Changing insurance *style*: consistent with the fact that our needs and attitudes may change over time, owners of VUL might find their risk tolerance moderating to the point where a No-Lapse UL or Whole Life *style* policy may be a better fit. Of course, those initially purchasing term insurance and finding their time-frames longer than anticipated may decide in favor of switching to a UL or VUL.

- Carrier financial condition: things change for life insurers as well. While there is less concern today than a decade ago, insurers occasionally fail and there's no equivalent of the FDIC to insure your cash values. As discussed in Section 1, Chapter 8: Financial condition is generally measured by the financial ratings of such companies as Moody's, Standard & Poors, Fitch, A. M. Best, and Weiss, and as a general rule one would want to buy a policy from a company that was in the top 2 categories of A. M. Best and no lower than a rating level "5" of the other rating agencies. From the standpoint of deciding if you should *leave* an insurer whose ratings have slipped, a one or two-step drop with one rating agency is not sufficient to suggest an immediate replacement. A qualified insurance professional can guide you through the process of making the subjective decisions surrounding a carrier's modest drop in financial ratings.

- Changes in budget: reduced circumstances could make it difficult to maintain a large policy with significant premiums, and a change in policy may well be the appropriate action.

- Even not liking how the insurance company's been treating you may be a consideration to switch to a company and/or agent you feel will give you more attention and better service. Just don't make the decision based on illustrated numbers!

Critical Questions to Help Clarify Considerations of Policy Replacement

1. What was the *purpose* for which you originally purchased the subject policy?

2. Does that *purpose* still exist?

3. Is the *amount* of the policy still appropriate? If there's still a need, but not as much, perhaps *reducing* the size of the policy will solve the problem prompting the replacement. On the other hand, if the need has increased since your last assessment and such increases are likely in the future, a recommendation to switch to No-Lapse UL's level death benefit is not likely to accomplish your objectives.

4. There's undoubtedly an increased premium requirement to maintain a current assumption policy if it was originally purchased based on best illustrated price. Can you *afford* this increased premium? Can the increased premium come from *capital*, freeing up the burden on your current income?

Practical Considerations – Do You Qualify for a New Policy?

Replacing a life insurance policy can involve a number of disparate facts and issues. Is the insured still insurable in an underwriting category at least as favorable as the original policy? Have there been any new avocations or activities that might result in a more costly rate class? Has a parent or sibling died since the first policy was underwritten? Has your income temporarily declined, potentially keeping you from purchasing as much insurance in the replacement policy as you already own? Do you understand that a current policy more than 2 years old is *incontestable* as to incorrect statements or death by suicide, and that a new policy will incur another 2-year period before it becomes incontestable?

The Replacement Questionnaire

The Society of Financial Service Professionals in Bryn Mawr, PA has produced an objective explanation and questionnaire for the purpose of assessing proposed policy replacements. A copy of the questionnaire will be found in the Appendix. When a policy replacement is recommended by an insurance agent, advisors and policy owners should consider asking the agent to fill out the form for additional disclosure and discussion items.

Chapter 17

No Lapse/Secondary Guarantee Universal Life Policy—a Special Case

A s reviewed in Section 1, Chapter 5, No Lapse/Secondary Guarantee Universal Life policies are a relatively new product type and are often proposed in support of policy exchanges when the original policy isn't performing to expectations. Often the numerical logic is impeccable: Why *wouldn't* you proceed to exchange your policy if a large, second-to-die policy is going to need a substantial increase in premium to bring it back to its *theoretical cash value* curve, and a No Lapse policy will guarantee the original coverage for an outlay *less than* that which the older policy requires?

No Lapse policies should be thought of as "lifetime term" with low (sometimes *very low*) guaranteed level premiums. Because premiums for these policies are often substantially less than Whole Life or even appropriately funded Universal Life, there will be little or no meaningful cash value available in a No Lapse/Secondary Guarantee Universal Life policy. This should not be viewed as a reason *not* to use such a policy, but rather it is the first in the list of *cautions*.

Issues to Bear in Mind

When considering No Lapse policies, especially in replacement, think about the following:

- The death benefit will not increase beyond the original amount, leaving no ability to offset the effects of inflation. Even an inflation rate of 3 percent will nearly double the cost of living in 20 years; this means today's death benefit will only do *half the job* 20 years from now.

- If legislation or circumstances render the insurance no longer necessary, the policy will likely have no long-term equity value to recoup the policy owner's investment. This is also significant if yet another evolutionary design comes along suggesting an exchange *out of* the No Lapse policy: there will be little or no exchange value to facilitate the move to a new policy.

- There is a concern that No Lapse policies are underpriced in a competitive frenzy within the life insurance industry, which if sold in too great a concentration to other lines of business, at the extreme, could lead to carrier failure. No Lapse insurance products are not so much guaranteed as they are backed by a guarantor. No Lapse caters to the (understandable) fears of premium inadequacy at the customer level, but potentially jeopardizes the relationship of insured to insurer at the industry level.

- Even large life insurance companies can fail. Both Executive Life and Mutual Benefit were among the 20 largest insurance companies in America in the late 1980s. By 1991, both had been declared insolvent and liquidated. Executive Life was highly rated within months of its collapse; Mutual Benefit was A+ (highest) rated by A.M. Best as late as 1989. Equitable—the third largest carrier in the United States—came close to failure before negotiating its acquisition by French insurer AXA.

- What's your reaction when you realize that the quoted price for an expensive service is for an amount that is clearly "too good to be true"? Even if you would proceed, would you do it if you were locking yourself into a lifetime contract from which you couldn't get out without a large loss?

No Lapse/Secondary Guarantee Universal Life (2UL) Illustrations

No Lapse illustrations look just like Universal Life illustrations; often the only way to determine from the *numbers* that there's a secondary guarantee is to look at the left-hand side (guaranteed values) of the numerical illustration pages. This reveals whether there is a continuing death benefit even after the cash value has fallen to $0. You'll also notice that there's very little cash value contained in the guaranteed columns, while the current columns seem to develop substantial cash value over the years. To determine which set of columns you should rely on, consider another question: If you were on the Board of Directors of an insurance company selling and managing No Lapse policies, and mindful of the fact that your company is "on the hook" for the death benefit no matter what happens to the cash value account, are there any reasons why you would declare a policy crediting rate *more* than the minimum guaranteed in the policy? Furthermore, and again mindful of the secondary death benefit guarantee, are there any reasons why you would charge any *less* than the maximum cost of insurance charges itemized in the policy? Of course not—and that's why consumers and advisors should always focus their attention on the guaranteed columns of No Lapse policies.

There Are Circumstances In Which 2UL May be Appropriate

Notwithstanding previous comments, for larger estate planning situations requiring significant amounts of life insurance, a certain percentage of No Lapse/Secondary Guarantee Universal Life may well be appropriate as a method of diversification of risks and premium allocations. In this instance, it would be appropriate to consider a *portfolio* of life insurance policies with an allocation of appropriately diversified policy types and insurance carriers. A typical allocation would allow for 20–30 percent of the total death benefit in No Lapse/Secondary Guarantee Universal Life.

Chapter 18

Case Examples

Many policies purchased in the 1980s and '90s are not meeting their illustrated expectations, especially if they were calculated on the basis of "best price." This is not so much a function of failed policies but of changing external economic factors (and significant volatility) that have adversely affected both interest-oriented policies—Whole Life, Universal Life, and Adjustable Life—as well as investment-oriented policies—Variable Universal Life and Equity Indexed Life. While a replacement policy may be suggested, policy owners should consider the larger picture: What can be done to put the current policy back on track? What will this cost, and what are the likely benefits? Once a realistic picture has been drawn, the possibility of replacement can then be considered in proper context.

Let's consider some typical case examples that might shed light on the often complex process of determining what to do about a life insurance policy that is not meeting its original expectations. Note that life settlements are specifically *not* addressed in these examples, because in each case there is the presumption of an ongoing need for life insurance.

Case 1: A Whole Life policy purchased eight years ago is now "costing too much." The policy owner wants and needs the coverage for the balance of her life, but as retirement approaches, she is concerned that the premium won't be affordable.

Facts: A 58-year-old physician purchased a $500,000 participating Whole Life policy in 1996. The annual lifetime policy premium is $20,576. The policy has accrued an additional $111,000 of paid-up additions death benefit, but the insured has determined that only the original $500,000 is necessary. Because this is a Whole Life policy and not flexible premium, there are limits to her ability to adjust the cash flow of future premium payments, and the insurance company will need to be involved in providing scenarios such as the following:

Option 1: Suspend cash premiums, instead making required premium payments from the cash value of paid-up additions for as long as they last. During this period, dividends continue to buy paid-up additions. When this source of premium payments is finally exhausted, resume premium payments *net of the then-current dividend.* Of course, because dividends are not guaranteed until paid, the following resulting schedule is subject to some modification.

Year	Cash Payment	Death Benefit
2004	0	$568,000
2005	0	$551,000
2006	0	$534,000
2007	0	$517,000
2008	0	$501,000
2009	0	$500,000
2010	$9,742	$500,000
2011	$10,285	$500,000
2012	$10,020	$500,000
2013	$9,785	$500,000
2018	$9,105	$500,000
2023	$7,250	$500,000
2028	$5,815	$500,000
2033	$4,840	$500,000

Option 2: A more dramatic option is to take the total death benefit of $611,000 and place the policy on a paid-up status.

This means the total death benefit will be immediately reduced to $325,000 and contractually have *no further premiums*. The paid-up policy will continue to earn dividends, which will slowly increase the overall death benefit as summarized below.

Year	Death Benefit
2004	$325,000
2005	$332,000
2006	$338,000
2007	$345,000
2008	$351,000
2013	$384,000
2018	$417,000
2023	$451,000
2028	$487,000

While this option presents a little considered option available in managing premiums for a Whole Life policy, it would not be the preferred approach unless there were no other alternatives, since this option substantially reduces the insured's initial death benefit. The insurance company should be consulted to determine the maximum reduction in death benefit that does not trigger a taxable gain.

Option 3: A final variation on these themes is to continue paying the full premium of $20,576 until the projection calculates that dividends can entirely take over the current premium payments. Using the current dividend scale, this would require paying *seven more* yearly premiums, making her 65 years old before dividends could take over the premium-paying burden for the balance of her life. The death benefit would continue to increase through 2010 to approximately $729,000, and would then begin to drop. For example, her death benefit at age 85 would be approximately $620,000 and at age 95 approximately $558,000.

Case 2: A second-to-die Universal Life policy in an irrevocable life insurance trust with anticipated funding premiums of $40,000 per year appears to have insufficient funding to sustain the policy for all years, but tax-effective gifts are limited.

Facts: In 1994, a healthy couple ages 53 and 51 purchased a Universal Life death benefit of $7,400,000, which—using the annual gift exclusion for joint gifts to two trust beneficiaries—was as much life insurance as $40,000 a year would provide. The interest crediting rate on their policy was 7 percent and the death benefit was calculated with that assumed rate.

The policy crediting rate is currently 4.75 percent (the guaranteed rate is 4.5 percent). An in-force analysis, including probability assessment, suggests the following (see graphic examples in Figures 18.1–18.5).

Life expectancy:	in a large group of couples of similar age, there's a 50/50 chance that at least one individual will be alive at age 93
Anticipated 10-year cash value:	$525,000 (the *theoretical cash value* curve)
Actual 10-year cash value:	$483,000
2004 policy statement in-force duration:	age 93
Illustration analysis earliest lapse:	age 88 (see Figure 18.1)
Probability analysis earliest lapse:	age 85
Probability policy will sustain to age 100:	5 percent
New funding premium to meet 90 percent probability test:	$100,000
Average death benefit at life expectancy with $100,000 funding premium:	$8,600,000
Average death benefit at age 100 with $100,000 funding premium:	$11,900,000 (see Figure 18.2)

Figure 18.1 In-force policy will lapse at age 88 with current 4.75% crediting rate and $40,000 funding premium.

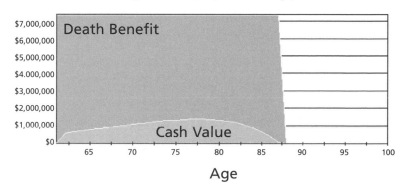

Figure 18.2 Undulating interest rate probability study suggests this result with $100,000 funding premium.

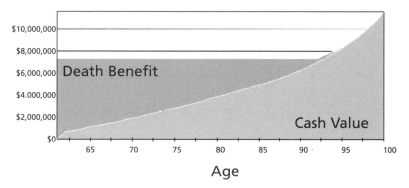

Figure 18.3 Continue $40,000 annual funding premium, reduce the death benefit to $4,000,000, and adjust the policy so it returns to its *theoretical cash value* curve.

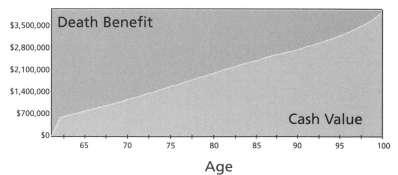

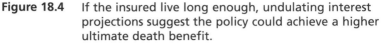

Figure 18.4 If the insured live long enough, undulating interest projections suggest the policy could achieve a higher ultimate death benefit.

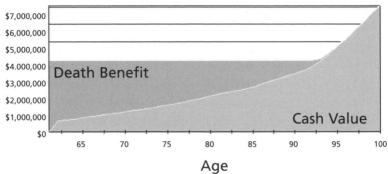

Figure 18.5 Use $1 million of the couple's lifetime exemption to make a one-time deposit to the policy; continue the $40,000 annual premium; resume the *theoretical cash value* curve.

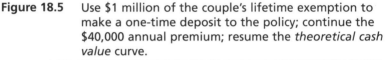

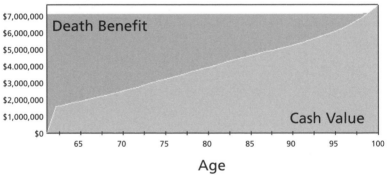

Option 1: Increase funding premium as presented. Even though eligible annual gifts could increase to $44,000 in 2004, the grantors were definitely *not* anticipating a 150 percent increase in their gifts—nor can they increase the gift to that level without using their lifetime exemption.

Option 2: Reduce the death benefit to $4 million, adjusting the policy so it returns to its *theoretical cash value* curve (see Figure 18.3). If the insureds live long enough, undulating interest projections suggest the policy could achieve a higher ultimate death benefit (see Figure 18.4).

Option 3: Use $1 million of the couple's lifetime exemption to make a one-time deposit to the policy, continue the $40,000 annual premium, and resume the *theoretical cash value* curve (see Figure 18.5).

Option 4: Exchange the Universal Life policy for a No Lapse/Secondary Guarantee Universal Life policy. If the couple's health is still good, as much as $3.8 million might be supported with the original $40,000 annual premium. Maintaining the full $7.4 million death benefit would require $109,000 with no possibility of an increased death benefit at older ages. Based on these figures, a replacement would not benefit this situation.

Case 3: A large Variable Universal Life policy in an Irrevocable Life Insurance Trust with funding premiums of $150,000 (originally calculated at a conservative 8 percent per year) has had significant losses in the all-equity subaccounts, and a current in-force illustration indicates that the premium is unlikely to sustain the policy to the insured's life expectancy. While only based on a five-year investment result, the trustees are nervous.

Facts: In early 2000, a healthy 60-year-old woman purchased a $10 million Variable Universal Life death benefit. Her irrevocable life insurance trust had substantial financial resources so that annual gifts were not necessary to support the policy. The initial funding premium of $150,000 has been paid into the policy for the last five years.

An in-force analysis—including probability assessment—suggests the following (see graphic examples in Figures 18.6–18.10):

Life expectancy:	in a large group of women of similar age, there's a 50/50 chance she will be alive at age 91
Anticipated 5-year cash value:	$620,000 (on the *theoretical cash value* curve)
Actual 5-year cash value:	$280,000

2005 policy statement in-force duration:	age 89
Illustration analysis earliest lapse:	age 88 (see Figure 18.6)
Probability analysis earliest lapse:	age 82
Probability policy will sustain to age 100:	50 percent (see Figure 18.7)
New funding premium to meet 90 percent probability test:	$220,000
Average death benefit at life expectancy with $220,000 funding premium:	$23,000,000
Average death benefit at age 100 with $220,000 funding premium:	$49,000,000 (see Figure 18.8)

Figure 18.6   In-force policy will lapse at age 88 with current assumed 6% average rate of return.

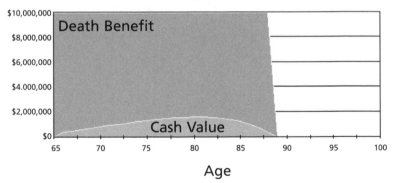

Figure 18.7

$10 Million Death Benefit
$150,000 Funding Premium

☐ Sustains
■ Does Not Sustain

Policy Performance Statistics			Investment Statistics	
Does Not Sustain:	150	50%	Average Arithmetic Mean:	10.95%
Sustains:	150	50%	Average Geometric Mean:	10.21%
Average positive ending account value:	$35,539,500		Average Standard Deviation:	15.59%
Earliest Age Policy Crashes:	82			
Average Death Benefit @ Life Expectancy:	$17,499,468			
Average Death Benefit @ Maturity:	$36,224,123			

Figure 18.8

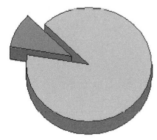

$10 Million Death Benefit
$220,000 Funding Premium

☐ Sustains
■ Does Not Sustain

Policy Performance Statistics			Investment Statistics	
Does Not Sustain:	31	10%	Average Arithmetic Mean:	10.84%
Sustains:	269	90%	Average Geometric Mean:	10.07%
Average positive ending account value:	$49,195,959		Average Standard Deviation:	15.66%
Earliest Age Policy Crashes:	87			
Average Death Benefit @ Life Expectancy:	$23,591,130			
Average Death Benefit @ Maturity:	$49,392,574			

Option 1: Increase funding premium as presented. There are sufficient resources within the trust to step up the funding.

Option 2: Reduce the death benefit to $7,400,000, adjusting the policy so it returns to its *theoretical cash value* curve (see Figure 18.9). If the insured lives long enough, randomized investment projections suggest that the policy could achieve a much higher ultimate death benefit (see Figure 18.10).

Figure 18.9 Maintain $150,000 funding premium, reduce the death benefit to $7.4 million, and adjust the policy so it returns to its *theoretical cash value* curve.

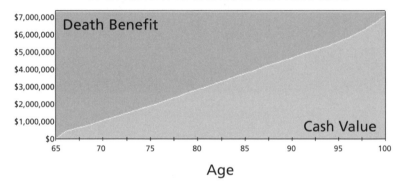

Figure 18.10 With randomized investment projections, the $7.4 million policy could achieve a higher ultimate death benefit.

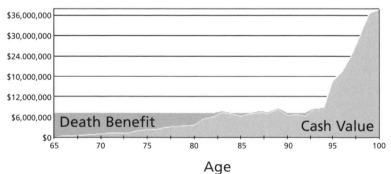

Option 3: Use $250,000 of trust resources to make a one-time deposit to the policy, continue the $150,000 annual premium, and resume the *theoretical cash value* curve.

Option 4: Exchange the Universal Life policy for a No Lapse/Secondary Guarantee Universal Life policy. If the insured's health is still good, a $10.1 million policy might be supported with the original annual premium. Based on these figures, a replacement would be of marginal benefit in this situation.

Chapter 19

Duties of Irrevocable Life Insurance Trust Fiduciaries

Third-party ownership arrangements are most often created to keep life insurance assets outside of the insured's estate. Aside from transfers of existing life insurance (for which there is a three-year "contemplation of death" delay in the policy being considered to have transferred for estate tax purposes), life insurance intended to be outside the estate should be acquired by a third-party owner. If more than one beneficiary is involved—or if the beneficiary is not of legal age or financially prudence—an Irrevocable Life Insurance Trust arrangement is ideal. In theory, a grantor considering such an arrangement would pick an appropriate trustee, meet with an attorney to draft and establish the trust, transfer funds on behalf of trust beneficiaries via "gifts of a present interest" arrangement, provide sufficient time for the beneficiaries to indicate that they choose not to exercise their annual right to withdraw all or a portion of the gift, and *then* acquire the life insurance policy. In the real world, the Irrevocable Life Insurance Trust is often the *last* detail to be attended to, and both personal and institutional trustees are often left with a fait accompli as to carrier, policy, and agent selection.

Because there are a number of constituents to the process initiated by trust grantors, it's worthwhile to consider some of the unique issues faced by attorneys, trustees, and beneficiaries that are not a *fiduciary* factor in personal ownership.

Attorney Issues

The estate planning attorney who drafts the insurance trust understands the importance of the life insurance policy along with its tax leverage, cost, and timing advantages. When a family member serves as personal trustee, the grantor and trustee both rely on the attorney for advice concerning the operation of the trust.

The attorney may be expected to assist the grantor in a number of ways:

- Selection of a life insurance agent and/or insurance company

- Determination of an appropriate amount of life insurance

- Selection of a suitable guaranteed or non-guaranteed death benefit product based on the trust's objectives and the grantor's risk tolerance

- Review of non-guaranteed policy sales illustrations for premium adequacy

- Confirmation of the annual or periodic trust and policy administration activities

Subsequently, if the trust objectives change or the life insurance policy is underperforming its expected values, the attorney may assist the trustee and beneficiaries in evaluating restructure options. The services of a "trust protector," who is often an attorney, are becoming popular with trust beneficiaries who seek to objectively monitor the trust management performance of a corporate trustee. Monitoring includes a review of trust-owned life insurance investments and stress testing different remediation and restructure options, if needed. However,

> ...if an attorney renders advice about the selection of an insurance product and the product does not live up to the client's expectations, the client may elect to sue the attorney for any damages incurred... The claimed damages may be with respect to the carrier becoming insolvent after the policy purchase, payment of additional premiums beyond a "promised" maximum

time period, or loss of favorable contract terms available under the non-selected policy, inter alia.[1]

Trustee Issues

The Prudent Investor Rule measures trustee prudence in terms of the process by which investment decisions are made—without the benefit of 20/20 hindsight. It instructs a trustee to design and actively carry out a reasoned investment strategy that will fit within the trust's unique purposes and the expectations of the beneficiaries to make the trust property productive. "Under the Prudent Investor Rule, fiduciaries must undertake investment strategies that best achieve the objectives for which private trusts are created, even if the trust document is silent as to the expected duties of the trustee."[2] It would be imprudent if the "process" were not in writing—covering investment policy (as appropriate) and policy management.

Yet a recent article in *Trust & Estates* found that more than 80 percent of professional trustees have no guidelines or procedures for handling trust-owned life insurance, and an overwhelming 96 percent had no policy statements on how to handle life insurance investments.[3]

The trustee has sole responsibility to determine whether the life insurance policy is suitable to achieve the Trust's objectives and, if not, how the policy should be restructured to do so. The trustee may choose between guaranteed and nonguaranteed policies, but if a nonguaranteed policy is selected, the trustee *must* affirm its premium adequacy evaluation and policy management capabilities to the grantor, obtain approval to assume this risk, and affirm that its acceptance analysis achieves the trust's objectives.[4] More subtle, but no less significant than policy performance management responsibility, is the trustee's duty to manage concentration risk. A life insurance policy owned in an insurance trust is, by its very nature, a concentrated asset. The decision of a professional trustee to assume concentration risk is difficult to defend unless it furthers the intent of the grantor and the decision process is demonstrably informed, clearly documented, and communicated to the parties at risk.[5]

Finally, with due consideration to a client's reasonable expectations, it is the duty of every professional fiduciary to advance best practice solutions for all assets under management. Life insurance is a sophisticated estate management tool that defies conventional financial analysis. Obtaining an in-force policy illustration and conducting a current "Google" search on the insurance company's financial ratings is *not* going to be sufficient in today's litigious environment. Accordingly, life insurance held in trust must be managed with the assistance of equally sophisticated evaluation tools. Such tools must be legally defensible, academically justifiable, and administratively feasible.

Beneficiary Issues

Because the trustee's basic fiduciary duty is to maximize the probability of a favorable outcome to the trust beneficiary, a beneficiary should receive an annual report that confirms policy performance consistent with the trust's objectives and the trustee's funding risk criteria. The trustee has a duty to inform the beneficiary of trust investment performance, and especially a duty to warn the beneficiary in the event of adverse performance. Finally, a beneficiary should expect the trustee to objectively verify that scheduled premium payments are adequate to successfully sustain the policy for the insured's lifetime.[6]

The typical scenarios that adversely affect insurance trust beneficiaries include the following:

- The trustee lacks defensible Trust-Owned Life Insurance (TOLI)-specific management procedures.

- Trust objectives are not documented (and possibly not known).

- The trustee accepts a new policy without an actuarially certified evaluation of premium adequacy.

- The trustee fails to take remedial action when in-force illustrations document policy underperformance—or more critically—when an in-force illustration doesn't reveal a strong *likelihood* that the policy will underperform.

- The trustee does not take advantage of policy enhancements offered by the carrier.

- The trust's purpose changes and the policy is surrendered to the insurance carrier for its cash surrender value, rather than sold in the life settlement secondary market for its fair market value.[7]

How to Meet the Elevated Standards of the Prudent Investor Rule

From a trustee's perspective, consideration must be given to how fixed return and equity purchases are made. The Prudent Investor Rule is based on Modern Portfolio Theory, first introduced in 1952. Modern Portfolio Theory has profoundly shaped how institutional portfolios are managed, and motivated the use of passive investment management techniques—except for life insurance portfolios! As emphasized in this book, indeterminate premium policies need to be periodically assessed for premium sufficiency, especially if the funding premium was calculated by a policy illustration during a time favorable to interest rate (Universal Life) or investment return (Variable Universal Life) assumptions. These periodic assessments need—in order to be legally defensible—to go well beyond in-force illustrations, generally utilizing the probability analysis processes described in Chapters 13, 14, and 18, which in turn derive from Modern Portfolio Theory concepts.

Life Settlements

Life settlements are a credible restructure alternative for TOLI policies that are in serious jeopardy because of underfunding. While not a panacea, life settlements potentially represent an additional rescue and value enhancement alternative for underperforming, unsuitable, and *unnecessary* policies. As a result, it is important to select a broker experienced with TOLI who can access all qualified providers, represent trustees' best interests, and provide the requisite full disclosure.

Conclusion

This book sheds light on and contains plenty of facts about key aspects of today's high-tech life insurance products and issues. Advisors and consumers may use this information to make informed decisions about their needs for and implementation of this important financial tool.

Facts have always been the stock in trade of the professional life insurance agent. For many years we were the gatekeeper of information, and we gave it away for free with the expectation that if you were ultimately going to buy life insurance, you'd "buy it from me." More often than not, it's been the insurance agent who helped identify the key planning obstacles and motivated the client to seek legal and accounting counsel to establish a good estate or financial plan.

Yet today's ready access to a vast amount of information (and indeed direct delivery products)—primarily through the Internet—has fundamentally changed the role of the insurance agent. As Jim Anderson *the father* was depicted in *Father Knows Best*, he would be an ideal advisor for today's insurance buyers. He was good at listening to the concerns of those who were "hurting," helping them to identify their problems (and appreciate the consequences of *not* solving the problem). Generally he wouldn't just offer a solution; he applied his knowledge and life skills to crafting questions of his "clients" to promote emerging solutions. Even more important, he could motivate implementation while helping the client maintain the courage of his convictions. Whether he knew it or not, Jim Anderson presaged a consultative model for the life insurance agent, demonstrating that his true role (and potential for business success) lies in his ability to work with clients as a financial advisor, synthesizing the overwhelming amount of data and information and focusing the client on creating a decision making and implementation process that produces an effective solution.

Appendix 1

Risk Tolerance Assessment

This is a simple process to assess your tolerance for investment risk. While it isn't a substitute for the advice of a qualified investment advisor, it can be useful to provide you with a reference point for further discussions with your advisor.

In the following six categories, please read and respond to the statements and questions by circling the number next to the response that best applies to you. When you are finished, simply add up the numbers of your circled responses. This is your score. You'll find the scoring assessment in Chapter 7 along with suggestions about the types of life insurance policies with which you may be comfortable and that are compatible with your risk tolerance assessment score.

When I invest, here's what's important to me…

> **1. Preservation of principal is paramount**. In other words, I want to minimize my risk. If faced with the choice: getting a return OF my money is more important than a return ON my money.

> **2. Current income is important to me**, and my investments should be relatively safe.

> **3. Current income is important. However, I would <u>also</u> like to see the value of my investments reasonably increase over time**. I am willing to incur a moderate level of risk to achieve this objective.

4. Growth of the value of my investments is important. However, I would also like to have some current income. I am willing to expose my investments to a fair level of risk to achieve this objective.

5. Substantial growth over time is important to me. I do not need to generate current income. I am willing to incur a considerable level of risk to achieve this objective.

How much the value of an investment moves up and down is called *volatility* or *risk.* There is generally a greater potential for growth *in the long term* for more volatile investments than those that generate less volatility, *but* the more volatile investment may also produce greater losses. With how much *volatility* are you comfortable?

1. As little as possible. I want to focus on current income and stability of value even if it means that my total returns are relatively small.

2. Some. I am willing to accept occasional losses in value as long as my investments have some potential for growth over time.

3. Moderate. I am willing to take moderate risk as long as my investments have a greater potential for growth over time.

4. A considerable amount. I am willing to take substantial risk in pursuit of significantly higher total returns.

It's also important to consider the effect of inflation on different investment options you can make. Investments in which principal is very safe sometimes earn *less* than the prevailing inflation rate. This could result in the loss of purchasing power. With respect to your investment objectives, which of the following is most important?

1. My investments should be safe, even if it means my returns do not keep up with inflation.

2. I am willing to risk an occasional loss of investment value so that my investments may grow at about the same rate as inflation over time.

3. It is important that my investments grow somewhat faster than inflation. I am willing to accept some risk while trying to achieve this goal.

4. My investments should grow much faster than inflation. I am willing to accept considerable risk to try to achieve this goal.

I understand the value of my investments can fluctuate over time—based on the amount of risk I am willing to take. Losses in any one-year period that I would be prepared to accept are as follows:

1. Minimal Loss

2. -5% to -10%

3. -10% to -15%

4. -15% to -20%

5. -20% or more

Consider two different investments as pictured below: Investment A, which provides an average annual return of 5% with a minimal risk of loss of value; and Investment B, which provides an average annual return of 10% but a potential loss of 25% or more in any year. How would you divide your investment dollars?

1. 100% in Investment A and 0% in Investment B

2. 80% in Investment A and 20% in Investment B

3. 50% in Investment A and 50% in Investment B

4. 20% in Investment A and 80% in Investment B

5. 0% in Investment A and 100% in Investment B

Figure Appendix 1.1

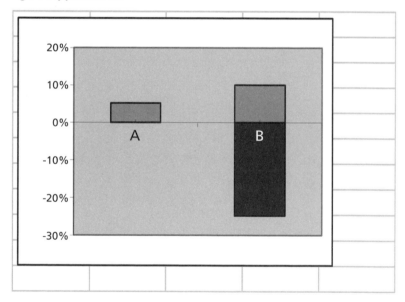

Finally, if you could choose only one of the five portfolios shown below, which would you select?

1. Portfolio A

2. Portfolio B

3. Portfolio C

4. Portfolio D

5. Portfolio E

Figure Appendix 1.2

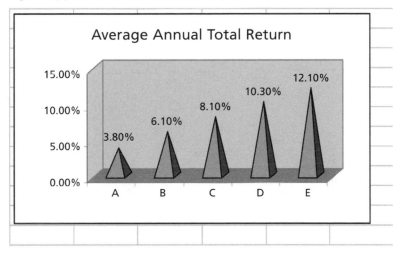

HIGHEST ANNUAL RETURN

A	B	C	D	E
14.7%	28.4%	34.1%	44.5%	127.6%

LOWEST ANNUAL RETURN

A	B	C	D	E
0%	-6.6%	-20.8%	-35.6%	-53.6%

Appendix 2

Replacement Questionnaire

The following information was developed by the Society of Financial Service Professionals to assist advisors and their clients to determine whether an existing policy should be retained or replaced. The responses are generally best determined by an insurance company or its agent.

Replacement Questionnaire (RQ)
A Policy Replacement Evaluation Form

For Chartered Life Underwriters (CLUs) and Chartered Financial Consultants (ChFCs):

Replacing an existing life insurance policy with a new one generally is not in the policyholder's best interest. New sales loads and other expenses, the new company's right to challenge a death claim during the suicide and contestability periods, changes in age or health, and the loss of important grandfathered rights are some of the obvious reasons that **most replacements cannot be justified.** On the other hand, there may be circumstances in which a replacement is in your client's best interest. The ethical agent will provide his or her client with the impartial information the client needs to make an informed decision, including why the client should not replace the current policy and/or how to modify the existing policy to accomplish the client's goals. The need for additional coverage is not, by itself, a justification for replacement.

This Policy Replacement Evaluation Form is designed to assist you in evaluating some of the facts and circumstances that a policyholder should take into consideration when addressing the possibility of replacing a life insurance policy. It can be used for both internal and external replacements. **The definition of "replacement" is much broader than the cancellation of one policy and the issuance of another.** The legal meaning of the word "replacement" is determined by state law and varies substantially by state. You should be familiar with your own state's definition of the word. However, for purposes of simplifying the definition, we may think of "replacement" in general terms as an action that eliminates the original policy or diminishes its benefits or values. Examples of this are policy loans, taking reduced paid-up insurance, or withdrawing dividends. Because no form can cover every possible situation, you may need additional material to enable your client to make a truly informed decision.

Please note that "illustrated" results in this form are always nonguaranteed. Keep in mind that different companies use different assumptions in preparing illustrations and that illustrations alone should never be used to compare policies. However, current in-force illustrations for the existing policy and current illustrations for the proposed policy must be provided to the client, showing the effects of applicable surrender charges. In situations where the current policy will be changed, but not terminated, comparisons should include in-force ledgers of the policy before and after the change, if available. Reduced scale illustrations (or illustrations with lower yield assumptions) should be provided on both existing and proposed policies to demonstrate volatility in the performance of nonguaranteed policy elements under different circumstances. The reduced-scale illustrations should be consistent with those required by the National Association of Insurance Commissioners model illustration regulations, when effective.

This form is intended for evaluation purposes. It is not a substitute for state replacement requirements. This form is not designed for direct use with clients. Furthermore, if either the existing or proposed policy is variable life insurance, use of this form with the client must be approved by your broker-dealer.

Replacement Questionnaire (RQ)

A policy replacement evaluation form to be completed by an insurance agent or carrier

A. 1. What does the policyholder want to achieve that the existing policy cannot provide?

_____

_____

_____

2. Has the current carrier been contacted to see whether the policy can be modified to meet the policyholder's objectives?

_____

_____

B. 1. Recognizing that the replacement of an existing policy generally results in the reduction of cash surrender value as a result of new acquisition costs, what is the cash surrender value of the following?

a. The original policy **immediately** before replacement _____

b. The original policy **immediately** after the replacement _____

c. The proposed policy **immediately** after the replacement _____

These cash surrender values should be obtained directly from the insurance carrier's policy owner service department and not from an illustration, because illustrations typically reflect end-of-year values.

2. Illustrations should **never** be the sole criteria for evaluating a replacement. Additionally, Illustrated Cash Values and Illustrated Death Benefits are **never** reliable predictions of future results. If these nonguaranteed values and benefits are the basis for considering a replacement, the agent should attempt to know and understand the underlying assumptions in the in-force illustration for the current policy, as well as in the sales illustration for the proposed policy. In addition to reviewing illustrations, the agent should attempt to

obtain an Illustration Questionnaire (IQ), which may be available directly from the companies or may be requested through the client. The agent and the client should be aware that there may be differences in the assumptions used by each company, which may render a comparison based on such illustrations invalid.

How many years are there until the proposed policy's cash surrender values and death benefits exceed those benefits in the current policy?

    a. Guaranteed Cash Surrender Values _____ years and subsequent.

    b. Guaranteed Death Benefits _____ years and subsequent.

    c. Illustrated Cash Surrender Values _____ years and subsequent.

    d. Illustrated Death Benefits _____ years and subsequent.

3. If the proposed policy is a variable life policy, what gross yield rate is being assumed? _____ Percentage: _____ %

    What is your justification for that rate? _____

    _____

    _____

C. 1. Describe the differences in the plans of insurance. _____

    _____

    _____

2. Describe any term riders or term elements (above the base policy). Include the ratio of the initial term amount to the total death benefit and any term rate guarantees that may or may not be included.

    Current policy: _____

    _____

    Proposed policy: _____

    _____

3. Other than term riders, what riders do the policies include?

Current policy: _____

_____

Proposed policy: _____

_____

4. How long is the initial death benefit **guaranteed** to be in force at the **illustrated** premium?

Current policy: _____ years. Proposed policy: _____ years.

5. What premium is necessary to **guarantee** coverage at initial/current levels for life?

Current policy: $_____. Proposed policy: $_____.

D. 1. Is there a potential taxable gain if the current policy is replaced?

 YES NO If yes, how is it to be managed?

_____

_____

2. If there is a taxable gain, **and if there is a loan,** how is the loan to be managed?

 The new policy will assume the existing loan.

 The loan will be repaid.

☐ The policy owner will recognize taxable income.

E. Is an Internal Revenue Code (IRC) Section 1035 exchange planned to preserve basis?

☐ YES ☐ NO

F. If a replacement is under consideration because a more favorable rate classification is available, has a reduction or removal of the rating on the existing policy been requested? If so, what was the result? If not, explain why such a request has not been made.

_____

_____

G. Does the proposed policy qualify as life insurance under IRC Section 7702?

☐ YES ☐ NO

H. What is the issue date of the current policy? _____

The following grandfathered features will be lost if the policy is replaced.

(See page **146–147** for an explanation of items 3–9.)

1. The current policy is incontestable by the insurance company.

☐ YES ☐ NO

2. The period has expired during which the insurance company can deny policy benefits in the event of the insured's suicide.

☐ YES ☐ NO

The current *life insurance policy* was issued on or before:			The current *annuity policy* was issued before:			The current *second to die policy* was issued before:		
	Yes	No		Yes	No		Yes	No
3. 8/06/63	( )	( )	6. 10/21/79	( )	( )	9. 9/14/89	( )	( )
4. 6/20/86	( )	( )	7. 8/14/82	( )	( )			
5. 6/20/88	( )	( )	8. 2/28/86	( )	( )			

I. 1. If the current policy is term, is a conversion to permanent insurance available?

☐ YES ☐ NO

2. If so, other than the suicide and incontestable provisions would a conversion to permanent insurance be more advantageous?

☐ YES ☐ NO

Explanation: _____

_____

_____

J. Financial Strength Ratings. Much has been made of ratings in the last few years; financial strength is important, but it is not the sole determining factor in selecting a life insurance company. A drop in ratings alone generally is not a sufficient reason to replace a policy. It is also important to know that there can be differences of opinion among rating agencies and that small differences in ratings generally are not significant. Furthermore, financial strength ratings are not necessarily indicative of policy performance. If reviewed with the client, a detailed explanation of the ratings must be provided in accordance with state regulations.

Current Company Rating (Rank)*	Proposed Company Rating (Rank)	Date and Source of Answer
A. M. Best (15 ranks)_____	_____	_____
Fitch Ratings (18 ranks)_____	_____	_____
Moody's (19 ranks)_____	_____	_____
Standard & Poor's (S&P) Claims Paying Ability** (18 ranks)_____	_____	_____

* For example, an AA rating from S&P is the third highest **rank** out of 18 possible ratings.

** S&P offers two rating services: Claims Paying Ability is on a par with the other services listed here; S&P's Qualified Solvency Rating is a much differently oriented rating and is inappropriate for use in this context.

K. Policy loans: Current Policy   Proposed Policy

   1. Gross rate: _____   _____

   2. Fixed or Variable?   _____   _____

   3. Permanent policies:
   Direct Recognition?   _____   _____

   4. Universal life, etc.
   a. Current spread?   _____   _____
   b. Is spread guaranteed? ❑ YES ❑ NO   ❑ YES ❑ NO

L. Additional remarks:

_____

_____

_____

_____

Reprinted and updated with permission from The Society of Financial Service Professionals, 270 S. Bryn Mawr Avenue, Bryn Maw, PA 19010

Grandfathered Features Explanation
Replacement Questionnaire, Question H

3. The current policy was purchased on or before August 6, 1963, so Internal Revenue Code (IRC) Section 264(a)(3), which limits deductions for interest indebtedness, does not apply. If the current policy has met the "four out of seven" test of IRC Section 264(c)(1), interest on indebtedness is deductible to the extent otherwise allowed by law. Personal interest deductions are generally denied for tax years beginning after 1990, irrespective of when the policy was purchased. IRC Section 163(h)(1).

4. The current policy was purchased on or before June 20, 1986. Certain policies purchased for business purposes after this date have a $50,000 ceiling on the aggregate amount of indebtedness for which an interest deduction is allowed. IRC Section 264(a)(4).

5. The policy was issued on or before May 20, 1988, and is not subject to Modified Endowment Contract rules. IRC Section 7702A. Substantial increases in the death benefits of grandfathered contracts after October 20, 1988, may cause the imposition of the Modified Endowment Contract (MEC) rules. H.R. Conf. Rep. No. 1104, 100th Cong., 2d Sess. (Technical and Miscellaneous Revenue Act [TAMRA] of 1988) reprinted in 1988-3 CB 595–596.

6. Variable annuity contracts purchased before October 21, 1979, are eligible for a step-up in basis if the owner dies before the annuity starting date. IRC Section 72; Rev. Rul. 79-335, 1979-2 CB 292.

7. An annuity issued before August 14, 1982, is subject to more favorable (basis out first) cost recovery rules for withdrawals. IRC Section 72(e). Such policies are not subject to the 10 percent penalty on withdrawals made before age 59 1/2. IRC Section 72(q)(2).

8. To the extent that contributions are made after February 28, 1986, to a deferred annuity held by a non-natural person (such as a business entity), the contract will not be entitled to tax treatment as an annuity. IRC Section 72(u).

9. A survivorship life policy issued before September 14, 1989, is not subject to the seven-pay MEC test if there is a reduction in benefits. IRC Section 7702A(c)(6).

This appendix is provided for educational purposes only. You should seek competent legal counsel before applying this to any specific situation.

Reprinted and updated with permission from The Society of Financial Service Professionals, 270 S. Bryn Mawr Avenue, Bryn Maw, PA 19010

Glossary

Accelerated Death Benefit:

A policy rider providing—under certain circumstances in which a physician certifies that the insured's death is imminent (generally within 1 year)—that a certain percentage of the death benefit can be paid out before the death of the insured.

Accidental Death Benefit:

A policy rider increasing the death benefit by a stated amount or percentage when death is certified as the result of an accident rather than from natural causes.

Account (also Accumulation) Value:

Especially applicable to Adjustable, Variable Universal and Universal Life, the account value is equivalent to the policy's cash value before the deduction of any applicable surrender charges when determining the policy's net *surrender value.*

Age at Issue:

Policies are approved and issued on a specific date. Insurers generally use the *nearest* age or the *last* age of the insured to determine the insured's age as of the issuance date.

Agent:

Individuals or businesses are licensed to sell life insurance by state Departments of Insurance, and are almost always considered to be defined as agents (rather than brokers), meaning that the sales person or entity has primary duties to the insurance company and *not* to the applicant. Agents may represent just one—or many—insurance companies, and are generally paid commissions by the insurer with whom the policy has been written.

Application:

A form provided by the insurer to obtain an individual's declaration of personal, occupation health, financial, and avocation information. The information provided by the insured (and typically completed by the agent) forms the basis on which an insurance company will make an offer to provide coverage. The application becomes a part of the legal contract of insurance, and the insurer is generally allowed to challenge misstatements if death occurs within 2 years of policy issue.

Assignment:

Since life insurance is property, it is possible to legally assign some or all rights in the policy to another party.

Assignee:

The individual or entity receiving rights in a life insurance policy assigned by the owner of the policy.

Attained Age:

The current age of the insured as measured from the age at the time the policy was issued.

Automatic Premium Loan Provision:

Generally applicable to fixed premium policies such as Whole Life, an "APL" provision will allow the insurance company to borrow the due and payable premium from cash values if the premium hasn't been paid after 31 days from the premium due date. This provision prevents an unpaid premium from putting the policy into a "lapse" condition.

Beneficiary:

The policy owner has the exclusive right to name the individual or entity to receive the death benefit upon proof of the insured's death. The beneficiary is generally not an irrevocable designation and can be changed by the policy owner.

Broker:

The terms "broker" and "agent" are defined by the various state Departments of Insurance. A broker (a term typically applied to those selling property and casualty insurance) is deemed to primarily represent the customer and not the insurance company. A broker generally represents more than one insurance company, and the broker's compensation is generally paid as a commission by the insurer with whom the policy has been written.

Broker-Dealer:

A licensed entity that is a member of the National Association of Securities Dealers (NASD) and registered with the Securities and Exchange Commission (SEC). A Broker-Dealer and its Registered Representatives are licensed to sell securities to the public. Appropriately registered individuals who are also licensed life insurance agents may sell security-oriented insurance products, including variable annuities and Variable Life insurance. Registered Representatives may also sell mutual funds.

Cash Surrender Value:

The value for which any policy with cash value can be surrendered. In a Whole Life policy, the surrender value is typically equal to the cash value. The surrender value may be less in indeterminate premium policies, depending on how long the policy was in force before surrender. (See Surrender Charge).

Cash Value:

The reserve created in *permanent* life insurance from the excess of premiums paid in early years compared to the amount the insurer needs to cover its annual death benefit liability. This reserve is important as the insured gets older, when the annual cost of the liability is significantly greater than the premium. The cash value is a policy owner asset. Indeterminate premium policies lapsed in the first 10–15 years may have a surrender charge, reducing the gross cash value.

Collateral Assignment:

Similar to Assignment, certain rights in a life insurance policy can be assigned to a third party, typically as security for a loan or other transaction. Collateral assignments are generally not made for a specified amount, but rather are defined "to the extent that his interest may appear." The assignment is registered with the insurer, and typically the assignee must prove to the insurer the amounts that are owed to it if and when the assignment collection criteria are met.

Contestable Clause (or Incontestable Clause):

Insurers typically allow themselves a period of two years from the date of issuing a policy, during which statements made on the application can be challenged for misstatement should death occur within that period. After the contestable period, the policy becomes incontestable except for application statements that can be proven as fraudulent.

Contract (Policy):

A life insurance policy is considered a legal contract between the insurer and the owner of the policy. Only the policy itself serves as the contract. Statements made by the agent and policy illustrations are *not* part of the contract of insurance.

Conversion:

Many term life insurance policies contain contractual provisions to exchange the policy for a more permanent form of insurance (such as Whole Life) without further evidence of insurability. Typically, conversion must occur before the term policy expires or by a certain date such as age 70.

Convertible:

A term used to describe a policy that contains a conversion provision.

Cost of Insurance:

Generally applicable to current assumption policies, monthly charges for mortality and other elements of insurer expense are assessed against the policy based on the insured's current age, the original rate class, and the current net amount at risk.

Current Assumption:

Life insurance policies that provide for contractually guaranteed policy credits and/or cost of insurance and other expenses, and for which higher policy credits (and/or lower cost of insurance and other expenses) *may* be used by the insurer at its discretion and experience.

Date of Issue:

The effective date of the policy as issued by the insurer.

Death Benefit:

The gross amount of cash benefit to be paid to the beneficiary of the policy upon certification of the insured's death. Actual benefits may be reduced by policy loans or policy assignments.

Death Claim:

When an insured dies, the policy owner will provide the insurer with proof of death (including a death certificate) and other information to cause the proceeds of the policy to be paid to the beneficiary.

Dividend:

Mutual insurers will typically accumulate surplus funds that can be designated as "divisible surplus" —funds that are not needed for the operation or reserves of the company. Divisible surplus is applied by formula to policies based on when they were sold and the amount by which such policies are deemed to have contributed to the surplus of the company.

Endow:

When a Whole Life or "endowment" policy's cash value is equal to the death benefit of the policy.

Evidence of Insurability:

At the time of application (and when certain changes are made to an existing policy), the insurer will establish standards for which it will issue a policy. Occupation, avocation, driving record, and medical records are among the typical factors that will be considered.

Excess Interest:

The difference (always positive) between the rate of interest an insurer actually pays and the guaranteed amount to be paid.

(Policy) Exchange:

Usually the result of a policy replacement, any potential taxable gain associated with terminating a policy can be deferred by qualifying the purchase of a new policy as an exchange under the provisions of Internal Revenue Code 1035.

Expense Charge:

A monthly charge paid to an insurance company based on various elements of the policy such as insured's attained age, original rate class, etc. Allowable charges are specified in the policy; at its discretion, the insurer may charge less than the contractual amount as circumstances allow.

Face Amount:

Also known as the stipulated amount, this is what will be paid at the death of the insured (or maturity of the contract, whichever occurs first). Additional amounts may be payable due to riders (e.g. accidental death benefit), through the application of additional amounts of insurance purchased by dividends, or through the return of an unearned premium.

Free-Look Provision:

Policyholders are generally given a 10–30 day opportunity to review the policy and, if they choose, return it for a full refund within the free-look period. If returned, the policy will be considered to be void from inception.

Funding Premium:

The appropriate term to describe premiums for policies that are designed without fixed premiums (see Indeterminate Premium). By adopting the modifier "funding," policyholders won't as readily believe that the premium quoted for Universal Life, Variable Universal and Adjustable Life conveys the same assurance it won't change as that of its Whole Life cousin.

Grace Period:

When a Whole Life policy premium comes due, the policy owner is generally given 31 days within which to make payment without jeopardizing the death benefit. Universal Life and Variable Universal Life policies generally allow 30-60 days for additional funding premiums to be paid if there's insufficient cash value to sustain the policy during the monthly calculation of expense charges and policy credits.

Gross Return:

Generally a term for Variable Universal Life, a gross return is the long-term average return assumed to be earned before deducting the management fees and other expenses described in the prospectus. Variable

Universal Life illustrations almost always assume a gross return, not to exceed the regulatory maximum of 12 percent. Annual fees can range from 0.25 percent to more than 2.0 percent of the account value.

Guaranteed Insurability Option:

Typically sold as a policy rider, it may be possible to assure the ability to purchase additional amounts of insurance at predetermined future intervals or ages without proving health and/or avocation evidence of insurability.

Indeterminate Premium:

A specific characteristic of Universal, Adjustable, and Variable Universal policies in which the premium is estimated but not guaranteed. It is the policy owner's responsibility to manage policy payments to ensure the sufficiency of the policy.

Insurable Interest:

When a policy is purchased, the buyer must have an economic interest in the life of the insured, or a demonstrable expectation of loss upon the death of the insured. A spouse is always considered to have an insurable interest. A business partner is similarly considered to have an insurable interest based on the economic value of the partnership. Your neighbor, however, cannot buy a policy on your life—even with your cooperation—unless a valid economic basis can be demonstrated. Once a policy is purchased, the policy owner is free to designate anyone he or she wishes as beneficiary. Policy ownership can be transferred after the policy has been issued, somewhat bypassing insurable interest statutes.

Insured:

The person whose life is covered by an insurance policy.

Interest Rate (Current and Guaranteed):

Each month, Universal, Variable Universal and Adjustable Life policies will credit an interest rate to the policy, which at a minimum is established by the policy (guaranteed rate), but which may exceed the minimum rate based on company discretion, experience, and management interest rate policy (current rate). The current rate is generally not itself guaranteed for any period beyond the current monthly accounting period.

Lapse:

For a Whole Life or term policy, the termination of an insurance policy resulting from non-payment of premiums within the specified premium payment grace period. A policy provision electing Automatic Premium Loan or a settlement option might allow a Whole Life policy to sustain beyond the grace period. For Universal, Adjustable or Variable Universal Life, a lapse will occur during the monthly accounting of expense charges and policy credits if the account value balance is $0 or less. Some insurers will consider a policy lapsed if the monthly accounting falls below $0 based on the cash surrender value. If a policy is in a lapse status, a grace period (typically 30–60 days) will generally apply to allow the policyholder to put more money into the policy.

Level Premium:

Generally refers to the initial period of a term policy in which the premiums are both guaranteed and constant. At the end of the initial period, premiums will generally increase annually and at a significantly higher rate than the level premium.

Life Expectancy:

Life expectancies are measured within large groups of people of similar age and gender. Newborn children born in America in 2005 have an average life expectancy to age of 77.4, which means that out of a group of 1,000,000 such infants, 500,000 will die before that age, and 500,000 will survive to at least that age. A surviving individual at age 77.4 might have another 12 years of life expectancy. Average life expectancies have been rising, but to some degree this statistic is affected by improving infant survival rates during their first year of life.

Life Settlement:

When a term policy comes to the end of its original duration and/or it is (ideally) no longer needed, policy owners are accustomed to simply "lapsing" the policy; with term, of course, there is no cash surrender value. But individuals over the age of 70 with deteriorating health who own such insurance might find that the policy is worth as much as 25 percent of its *death benefit* to financial enterprises that seek to purchase and maintain such policies until the insured's death.

Maturity Date:

A life insurance policy will typically mature at age 95 or 100, although newer policies may provide for contract maturity as far out as age 120. When the policy matures, all accrued benefits as described in the policy are paid. Some insurers allow the deferral of matured values until the insured's actual death.

Modified Endowment Contracts (MEC):

Modified Endowment Contracts (MEC) are the result of paying too much funding premium into a Universal, Variable Universal, or Adjustable Life policy in too short a period of time (usually in the first 7 years). Typically only the insurance company can accurately determine whether payments into a life insurance policy risk run the risk it will become "a MEC." Once the MEC condition has been reached, it cannot be reversed. While the tax status of death benefits is unaffected, the practical effect of a MEC is to cause any lifetime withdrawals of cash value to be taxed on a "last in / first out" basis, generally not as favorable as the non-MEC tax treatment of a life insurance policy. There is also a 10% tax penalty for withdrawals from a MEC policy before the age of 59 ½.

Medical Information Bureau (MIB):

All responses on a policy application are subject to submission to the MIB, an independent entity that collects and stores medical data on life and health insurance applicants. This information is exchanged among member insurance companies with written authorization of the insured. Its purpose is to prevent applicant fraud and to help insurers discover withheld information that may be contained in the database.

Misstatement of Age:

One of the primary factors affecting the cost of life insurance is your age. If age is misstated and it is not discovered until death of the insured, the insurance company has the contractual right to adjust the death benefit to reflect the face amount that would have been paid with the corrected age and actual premiums paid. Misstatement of age and/or gender is generally not subject to the 2-year contestability clause limitation.

Monthly Anniversary:

Because Adjustable Life, Universal and Variable Universal Life policies account for expenses and credits on a monthly basis, the monthly anniversary is the same day of each month as the policy anniversary date.

Net Amount at Risk:

The difference between the gross death benefit and the cash value. The net amount at risk should be largest in the early years and progressively diminish as the insured gets older, compensating for the lower risk cost when young and the higher risk cost as one gets older.

Net Cash Surrender Value:

A life insurance policy's cash surrender value less any outstanding loans or surrender charges.

Net Return:

Insurers selling and managing Universal Life, Adjustable Life and Current Assumption Whole Life policies will declare, from time to time, a policy cash value interest crediting rate not less than the guaranteed minimum specified in the policy. Both the declared and the minimum crediting rates are *net* of investment management expenses.

Nonforfeiture Values:

For more than 100 years, insurance regulators have required that permanent life insurance policies have certain equity rights, even when the policy might lapse due to non-payment of premiums. Nonforfeiture values include cash value net of loans, reduced paid-up life insurance, and extended term insurance.

Option A/Option B Death Benefits:

Universal Life, Variable Universal, or Adjustable Life policy owners may elect a level death benefit (Option A) or a death benefit that consists of the death benefit stipulated on the specifications page of the policy *plus* the cash value account (Option B).

Other Insured Rider:

An optional policy rider that provides specified amounts of term insurance on the life of a spouse or child of the primary insured.

Owner (Policy Owner):

An individual or entity (Trust, business, charity, etc.) that owns an insurance policy. Even if an individual, the owner isn't necessarily the insured. The policy owner has all typical rights of ownership, including the right to designate and change the beneficiary, borrow from the policy, or withdraw cash (Universal or Variable Universal life).

Participating Policy:

A participating policy is typically issued by a mutual life insurer whose profits (surplus) are for the benefit of its policyholders. If there is sufficient surplus to be paid out amongst the current policyholders, they will be paid out as dividends which can be taken in cash, reduce the premium due, or enhance the policy.

Payor:

Typically the policy owner, the payor is the person or entity making premium payments on a life insurance policy. In certain situations (e.g. divorce decrees), the insured may have a legal obligation to pay premiums without having an ownership right in the policy on his life.

Permanent Life Insurance:

Policies sold for lifetime needs. Policies may have specified premiums, wherein the insurer guarantees the sufficiency of the policy, or indeterminate premiums, requiring policy owners to manage the economics and the risk of maintaining the policy throughout the insured's lifetime.

Planned Periodic Payment:

Adjustable, Universal and Variable Universal Life policies do not have specified premiums; it is up to the policy owner to determine how much to pay. The application will ask for a specific amount to be billed on a periodic basis (monthly, quarterly, semi-annual, or annual), and this amount can generally be changed at the policy owner's direction.

Policy (Contract):

The basic written agreement between the insurer and the policy owner. The policy, together with the application and all endorsements and attached papers, constitutes the entire contract of insurance. The policy illustration is specifically *excluded* from the contract.

Policy Anniversary:

An anniversary of the policy issue date.

Policy Date:

The date on which coverage becomes effective, as typically shown on the policy specifications page.

Policy Lapse:

Unless other nonforfeiture provisions are elected, a Whole Life policy may *lapse* if the stipulated premium is not paid within 31 days of the policy anniversary date. An Adjustable, Universal or Variable Universal Life policy will lapse if the cash value account falls to $0. Typically, a grace period will be allowed to pay more premium and at least temporarily rescue the policy from lapse.

Policy Loan:

An amount of money somewhat less than the net cash surrender value of a life insurance policy that can be borrowed by the policy owner. The policy loan does not have to be repaid, but interest (as specified in the policy) will be charged and the total loan plus unpaid interest will be subtracted from policy proceeds if the loan is outstanding at the time of death or surrender of the policy.

Policy Year:

Life insurance policies are measured year-by-year from the data of inception. A policy purchased 10 years ago is in its tenth policy year.

Policy Owner/Contract Owner:

An individual (or entity) owning a life insurance policy. The policy owner may or may not be the insured or the beneficiary. While a third party may be the premium payor by special agreement, the policy owner typically pays the premium and has all rights of policy ownership such as taking policy loans or changing the beneficiary.

Premium:

State insurance regulators uniformly require the term "premium" to describe payments made on behalf of life insurance policies. However, only Whole Life and term policies have conventional "premiums"—

defined payments which maintain coverage for a certain period as described in the policy. Payments made on behalf of Adjustable, Universal, and Variable Universal policies aren't really premiums in the conventional sense, since the policy can lapse at any time when account values fall below $0.

Premium Mode:

The frequency of premium payments, ranging from monthly, quarterly, semi-annual, and annual. Whole Life and term policy premiums are almost always quoted on an annual premium basis, and more frequent modal payments will include an implied interest charge.

Rated / Rate Class:

Insureds are "rated" based on health, occupation, avocation, and other lifestyle considerations. Individuals with above average "ratings" are generally classified as "preferred," and all things being equal will pay lower premiums than their "standard" or "sub-standard" friends. While otherwise healthy smokers are generally classified in a "standard" category, smokers will pay significantly more for the insurance portion of their policies than a non-smoker.

Reinstatement Provision:

Most life insurance policies will grant the policy owner the right for a limited period of time to reinstate a policy after it has lapsed. Evidence of insurability will generally be required, as well as back premiums and interest.

Replacement:

Often defined by state insurance regulation, a replacement is typically deemed to have been made when an agent solicits a new policy in exchange for an old one, or when cash values are borrowed to support a new policy purchase. Policy replacement is generally inappropriate without certain mandated disclosures and, in some states, forms and notification to the original insurance company.

Policy Exchange:

Usually the result of a policy replacement, any potential taxable gain associated with terminating a policy can be deferred by qualifying the purchase of a new policy as an exchange under the provisions of Internal Revenue Code 1035.

Secondary Guarantee:

Seemingly contrary to principals of insurer financial prudence, some life insurance companies today sell policies that are guaranteed to pay a death benefit *even if the cash value falls to $0*. Rather than the cash value sustaining the policy, the insurer provides a *secondary* guarantee that it will pay the death benefit regardless of policy reserves.

Suicide Provision:

Agatha Christy was wrong! Suicide is covered by a life insurance policy *after* the (generally two-year) contestable period. If death is the result of suicide before the contestable period has passed, the insurance company is obligated only to pay a refund of premiums paid.

Surrender:

The policy owner's right to terminate policy coverage in exchange for the policy's cash surrender value or other nonforfeiture values.

Surrender Charge:

Typically applicable to Adjustable, Universal, and Variable Universal policies, a generally declining schedule of charges against the cash value may be imposed on the policy for a certain number of years from policy inception if the policy is surrendered, the death benefit is reduced, or in some instances, the surrender charge is taken into account in the monthly calculation to determine if the policy is still in force.

Surrender Value:

The value for which any policy with cash value can be surrendered. In a Whole Life policy, the surrender value is typically equal to the cash value. The surrender value may be less in current assumption Whole Life or indeterminate premium policies, depending on how long the policy was in force before surrender.

Survivorship Life Insurance Policies:

Policies covering two individuals—almost always husband and wife. The death benefit is contractually defined as payable only after the *second* of the two insureds has died.

Term Insurance:

Policies whose duration is specified in the policy, from 1–30 years, are typically referred to as "term" life insurance. Term policies may be renewable annually, renewable after certain increments of time, or may even be non-renewable after the policy "term." There is typically no cash value in a term policy, and the death benefit will be paid only if the policy is in force on the date of death. Modern term policy premiums are often guaranteed for an initial period, and then are subject to maximum renewal rates specified in the contract for whatever remaining period of renewal may be specified.

Transparency:

Whole Life is opaque as to its components. Nowhere in a typical illustration will the policy buyer see the various expenses of premium taxes, overhead, mortality expense, and profit margins; they are integrally and inseparably entwined into the calculation that results in specifying a premium that is guaranteed sufficient as long as it is paid. Adjustable and Universal Life is generally *transparent.* All of these expenses are discrete, and for most of them there is separate accounting. Variable Universal Life is the most transparent: The prospectus will specify each and every expense element. Some observers have erroneously assumed that, because premium taxes are specifically accounted for in a Variable Universal Life (and sometimes a Universal Life) policy, there are more "costs" associated with such policies, but this is *not* the case. Premium taxes, for example, are accounted for and paid by the insurer on all premiums whether they are specifically expressed in the policy or not.

Universal Life:

A term-of-art to describe flexible rather than fixed premium life insurance policies. Since there is no defined premium (other than a possible minimum premium in the first year or several years), it is the policy owner's responsibility to make certain that enough money is paid into the policy that it will stay in force as long as the insured is alive. Universal Life policy owners typically also have a contractual right to adjust the death benefit (requiring evidence of insurability if the death benefit is being increased) and to determine the amount and frequency of payments.

Valuation Date:

A date on which policy account values—typically in variable policies—are contractually determined.

Variable Universal Life:

A universal life insurance policy providing for flexible premiums and death benefits, but for which the policy owner has the opportunity and responsibility to designate how the policy premiums will be invested in separate investment accounts. The cash surrender value typically conveys *no* guarantees, and will fluctuate with the market value of the separate "sub-account" investment portfolio. The policy owner bears the risk of poor fund performance.

Waiver of Monthly Deduction:

A rider that waives monthly cost of insurance charges in an Adjustable, Universal, or Variable Universal life insurance policy for a period of disability as outlined and defined in the policy.

Waiver of Specified Premium:

A rider that waives premiums in a Whole Life or term insurance policy—or waives a planned premiumx in an Adjustable, Variable or Universal Life policy—for a period of disability as outlined and defined in the policy.

Whole Life Insurance:

A plan of insurance that covers the insured for life with fixed, level premiums payable for his or her entire lifetime. Under a Whole Life policy, premiums cannot be increased and the policy is guaranteed to stay in force for as long as the insured is living (and as long as the stipulated premiums are paid within the insurer's grace period).

Notes

Chapter 1

[1] Federal Reserve Prime Lending Rates, released June 9, 2003.

[2] *Federal Reserve Bulletin*, January 1977. *Statistical Abstract of the United States*, 1976. *Insurance Facts*, Insurance Information Institute, New York.

[3] Federal Reserve Prime Lending Rates, released June 9, 2003.

[4] American Council on Life Insurance (ACLI), *Life Insurance Fact Book*, 1994.

[5] A.M. Best's *Agents Guide to Life Insurance Companies*, 1989 edition.

[6] A.M. Best's *Agents Guide to Life Insurance Companies*, 1989 and 2004 editions.

[7] American Council on Life Insurance (ACLI), *Life Insurance Fact Book*, 2001.

[8] LIMRA International.

Chapter 2

[1] 2001 Commissioner's Standard Ordinary (CSO) Mortality Table, American Academy of Actuaries, as adopted by the National Association of Insurance Commissioners (NAIC).

[2] American Council of Life Insurance (ACLI), *Life Insurer's Fact Book*, 2001.

[3] American Association of Fundraising Councel (AAFRC) Trust for Philanthropy, publishers of *Giving USA*, available at www.aafrc.com.

Chapter 4

[1] The actuarial statistics discussed in this chapter are derived from the 2001 Commissioners Standard Ordinary (CSO) Mortality Table developed by the America Academy of Actuaries, as adopted by the National Association of Insurance Commissioners (NAIC).

Chapter 5

[1] American Council of Life Insurers (ACLI) *Life Insurers Fact Book*, 2001.

Chapter 8

[1] Richard G. Clemens, *A New Look at Demutualization of Mutual Insurers*, www.insurance-finance.com/files/doc2.html, accessed on Nov. 1, 2004.

[2] LIMRA International.

Chapter 9

[1] 2001 CSO Mortality Table, American Academy of Actuaries, as adopted by the NAIC.

Chapter 10

[1] Life Insurance Illustration Questionnaire (IQ), The Society of Financial Service Professionals, Bryn Mawr, Pennsylvania; revised April 1996.

Chapter 11

[1] Occam's razor is a logical principle attributed to the medieval philosopher William of Occam (or Ockham). The principle states that one should not make more assumptions than the minimum needed. This principle is often called the principle of parsimony. It underlies all scientific modeling and theory building. It admonishes us to choose the simplest model from a set of otherwise equivalent models of a given phenomenon. In any given model, Occam's razor helps us to "shave off" those concepts, variables, or constructs that are not really needed to explain the phenomenon. Doing that makes developing the model much easier, and it reduces the chances of introducing inconsistencies, ambi-

guities, and redundancies. F. Heylighen, July 7, 1997, Principia Cybernetica Web site: http://pespmc1.vub.ac.be/OCCAMRAZ.html.

[2] A reinterpretation of Aristotle's *Poetics*.

[3] Process "undulates" projected returns on 10-year Treasury bond on the basis of historic rate movements.

[4] Historic, all-equity average return of 12.3 percent from 1964–2003.

[5] Historic, all-equity average return of 12.3 percent from 1964–2003 in which each monthly return is reduced approximately 30 percent.

Chapter 13

[1] U.S. Treasury 10-Year T-Bond Yield Forecast. Constant Maturity Rate. Available at http://forecasts.org/interest-rate/10-year-treasury-bond-yield.htm.

Chapter 15

[1] Alan H. Buerger, "Life Settlements Come of Age," *Trusts & Estates*, November 2002.

[2] Brian Brooks and Elizabeth Baird, "Clients May Hold Millions in Untapped Insurance Wealth, Study Finds," *On Wall Street*, November 2002.

[3] Alan H. Buerger, "Life Settlements Come of Age," *Trusts & Estates*, November 2002.

Chapter 19

[1] B.A. Christensen, JD, CLU "Lawyer Liability for Life Insurance Policy Selection," Real Property, Probate and Trust Law Section, American Bar Association Annual Meeting, August 1994.

[2] E. Randolph Whitelaw and Liz Colosimo, JD, "Best Practices for Trust-Owned Life Insurance (TOLI) Trustees," *TOLI Fiduciary*, 3rd Quarter 2004.

[3] Richard L. Harris and Russ Alan Prince, "The Problem with Trusts Owning Life Insurance." *Trusts & Estates*, May 2003.

[4] Ibid.

[5] Ibid.

[6] E. Randolph Whitelaw and Liz Colosimo, JD, "TOLI Risk Management—Guilty Without Proof of Innocence," Fiduciary & Investment Risk Management Association, Spring 2004 Newsletter.

[7] Ibid.

Resource
Guide

RECOMMENDED READING

The Life Insurance Handbook
By Louis S. Shuntich

Term Life insurance, Whole Life insurance, Variable and Universal Life insurance – the list of choices for insurance products continues to grow, along with the different uses and tax implications associated with each. Despite the dizzying pace of change in the industry, every financial professional must understand the different types of insurance available – and the considerations for purchasing them.

$19.95   Item# BC101x-1611783

Life Insurance in Action Set with 25Q
By Dearborn Financial Publishing

This text provides an understanding of the ways life insurance offers financial stability and protection against the financial constraints of death. It explains the many applications of life insurance products and how their flexibility allows them to cover a wide range of clients' needs.

$29.00   Item# BC101x-1834687

Life and Health Insurance, 13th Edition
By Kenneth Black and Harold D. Skipper

In this newly revised thirteenth edition, the authors continue their emphasis on combining current information about life and health insurance products and their uses with careful consideration of the environment. They also carry on approaching their presentation of life and health insurance simultaneously from the viewpoints of the buyer, the advisor, and the insurer. This outstanding book is an informative guide to all the ins and outs of life and health insurance.

$133.00   Item# BC101x-12530

New Life Insurance Investment Advisor: Achieving Financial Security for You and Your Family Through Today's Insurance Products, 2nd Edition

By Ben G. Baldwin

This book is one of the most authoritative resources on today's highly dynamic, versatile, and adaptable investment vehicle. It covers Term Life, Whole Life, Universal Life, Variable Life insurance – and more. Discover the benefits of each for various client scenarios and life goals – and learn how to apply them when building stable portfolios. From finding optimal insurance products for different life stages to innovative techniques for using the capital hidden in each policy – this is the definitive book on the topic.

$29.95   Item# BC101x-41593

Investment Guarantees: Modeling and Risk Management for Equity-Linked Life Insurance

By Mary Hardy

Whether you are involved with product design, marketing, pricing and valuation, or risk management of equity-linked insurance, this book has something for you. It combines the econometric analysis of these investment models with their applications in pricing and risk management. Filled with professional insights and proven techniques, this comprehensive guide is a valuable one-stop reference that will allow you to better understand the theory and practice behind modeling and risk management for equity-linked life insurance.

$95.00   Item# BC101x-956602

The Complete Guide to Compensation Planning with Life Insurance
By Louis S. Shuntich

Help your clients attract and retain high caliber employees with this new and compact reference guide. An ideal educational tool for today's information-hungry and time-strapped professional, this book includes an overview of the various compensation plans available, the many features each plan offers, and a summary of how they compare and can be applied to different scenarios.

$29.95   Item# BC101x-1611782

Passtrak Life Insurance: License Exam Manual
By Dearborn Financial Publishing

This course surveys life insurance principles and concepts common to all state producer licensing exams. It is intended as a comprehensive introduction to life insurance. Topics include contract law, life insurance policies, premiums and proceeds, underwriting and policy issue, group life insurance, annuities, retirement plans, and more. The book further contains lesson objectives and special notes. It is clear, complete, up-to-date, and consists of revised forms and the NAIFA Code of Ethics. An index is included to make this text more useful as a study and reference tool.

$26.00   Item# BC101x-758345

▲▲▲▲▲▲

Many of these books, along with hundreds of others, are available at a discount from FP Books.
To place an order, or find out more, visit us at

www.fpbooks.com
or call us at
1-800-272-2855 ext BC101

Free 2 Week Trial Offer for U.S. Residents From Investor's Business Daily:

FREE 2 WEEK Trial Offer

INVESTOR'S BUSINESS DAILY

Power Processors Light Up Internet Even When All The Lights Go Out

INVESTOR'S BUSINESS DAILY will provide you with the facts, figures, and objective news analysis you need to succeed.

Investor's Business Daily is formatted for a quick and concise read to help you make informed and profitable decisions.

> To take advantage of this free 2 week trial offer,
> e-mail us at customerservice@fpbooks.com
> or visit our website at www.fpbooks.com where
> you find other free offers as well.
>
> You can also reach us by calling 1-800-272-2855
> or fax us at 410-964-0027.

Insurance Solutions Reports

Insurance Solutions Reports
provide objective answers to
key issues surrounding the
purchase and management
of life insurance:

How MUCH life insurance do I need?

With what TYPE of policy will I be most comfortable?

What's my life insurance STYLE?

How much should I PAY for my policy?

From which INSURANCE COMPANY should I buy my policy?

How is my policy DOING? Should I replace an "under-performing" policy or stay the course with what I have?

The Ethical Edge Inc.
www.EthicalEdge.biz/Secrets

EXPERT

INDEPENDENT

OBJECTIVE

FEE-ONLY

Second Opinion Analytical Services

Low interest rates and a volatile stock market have adversely affected Universal and Variable Universal life insurance policies. If "premiums" were solved assuming long-term crediting rates (UL) or investment returns (VUL) of more than 6%, it's advisable to evaluate the long-term likelihood the policy can achieve the policy owner's objectives.

● It's estimated that more than half of the UL and VUL policies owned in Irrevocable Life Insurance Trusts will have a hard time sustaining to life expectancy without adjusting the funding premium. Whole Life policies with blended term or vanishing premiums may also be unable to meet their original intention without re-evaluation.

● VUL policies funded with 10% assumed rates of return may have less than a 50% probability of sustaining significantly past life expectancy.

Re-evaluating Whole Life, UL and VUL life insurance policies is as important as the periodic review of an investment portfolio.

The Ethical Edge Inc.
www.EthicalEdge.biz/Secrets

EXPERT
INDEPENDENT
OBJECTIVE
FEE-ONLY

About the Author

RICHARD M. WEBER, MBA, CLU
TEL & FAX 760 652 4008 ❖ DICK@ETHICALEDGE.BIZ
WEB: ETHICALEDGE.BIZ

Dick is known as one of the life insurance industry's leaders for his work in insurance company and product Due Care. For 25 years a successful life insurance salesman and 20-year life member of the MDRT, he joined Merrill Lynch Insurance Group, and from late-1993 to the end of 1995 was Vice President and Manager of Client Education and Field Development. For his two year "tour" in upper management with a life insurance carrier, his responsibilities included developing communication programs which enhance client understanding of insurance products and reconciling product performance against product expectations. Since then, Dick founded and is President of The Ethical Edge, Inc., providing policy owners with "second opinion" assessments of life insurance as well as conducting training and consulting services that help empower both agents and their clients to explore and view life insurance in the broader context of financial planning. During this same period, Dick was a co-developer of *Dynamic Insurance Solutions* and *Historic Variability Module* – computer-based tools that have begun to revolutionize the way advisors and their clients view life insurance products.

Among his various teaching activities, Dick served for 11 years as an Instructor of Insurance at the University of California at Berkeley's Program in Personal Financial Planning and served as Adjunct Professor of Ethics at the American College in Bryn Mawr, Pa. from 1993 to 1998.

Dick holds an M.B.A. from the University of California at Berkeley with a specialty in Insurance and Finance. He was designated a Chartered Life Underwriter in 1974 by the American College. He has served as President of both the local Life Underwriter and the local CLU Chapters in the San Francisco Bay Area, has been a member of the Association for Advanced Life Underwriting, and has served as a Regional Vice President of the Society of Financial Service Professionals.

For a publication record of 150 issues, Dick's monthly Due Care column for *Life Insurance Selling* was one of the few agent-focused tutorials for ethical selling during the industry's most turbulent decade . He is also a contributing author to *Managing Sales Professionals,* a text for management training published by The American College. Other periodicals in which Dick's writings have appeared include *Probe, The Society Page, The CLU Journal, Trust & Estates,* and *Best's Review.* He is also the author of a (self-published) book for life insurance professionals: *The Ethical Edge: How to Compete with Your Integrity Intact (and Still Get the Sale!).* Derived from Dick's articles, the book's primary focus deals with understanding carrier solvency, interpreting carrier ratings, and determining the adequacy of life insurance proposal illustrations. His newest book due to be published Summer 2005, *Revealing Life Insurance Secrets: How the pros pick, design, and evaluate their own policies,* is directed at advisors and financial service professionals.

Dick has given presentations to the CLU Institute, the Million Dollar Round Table, the Society of Financial Service Professionals, AICPA – PFP Technical Forum, NYU Institute on Federal Taxation, the Association for Advanced Life Underwriting, Trusts & Estates Educational Forum, LIMRA, the International Association of Financial Planners, the Society of Actuaries, the American Bar Association, Nebraska Continuing Legal Education, and the College for Financial Planning. He has also created numerous customized programs for insurance companies and their agents, and for 6 years chaired the "Life & Annuities Market Conduct" symposium sponsored by International Business Conferences USA. In 1998 Dick's influence spread to Asia where, at the invitation of the Singapore College of Insurance, he conducted a special ethics seminar for agency managers.

In 1993, Dick represented the Society of Financial Service Professionals in an unprecedented series of 25 Due Care Workshops presented around the country. The Workshops introduced to agents and allied professionals the

American Society's Life Insurance Illustration Questionnaire ("IQ"). The Workshops also focused on what the agents can do with the information contained in their carrier's response to the "IQ" and how to return to a more fundamental, ethical, and educational form of selling the life insurance product.

In 1999, Dick once again represented the Society of Financial Service Professionals in a "reprise" 25-city tour with his seminar "The Ethical Edge: The Agent's and Adviser's Guide to Surviving and *THRIVING* in Today's Compliance Environment." The seminar discusses the "top-down" process of IMSA and offers to agents a complementary "bottom-up" set of ethical sales standards with which to conduct their business.

For 6 years Dick served as chairman of the Society's "IQ" Task Force, which has been responsible for producing the "IQ", the Replacement Questionnaire ("RQ"), and the Variable Insurance Questionnaire ("VIQ"). Dick has also chaired the Society's Market Conduct Task Force and has served as moderator of many of the Society's Video Teleconference education programs. On behalf of the Foundation for Financial Service Professionals, he has written and presented 6 internet-delivered educational video segments on the subject of "Retirement Planning for Baby Boomers."

Most recently Dick has been certified as a Qualified Independent Assessor for the Insurance Marketplace Standards Association (IMSA), established in 1997 by the American Council of Life Insurance (ACLI) for the purpose of affirming high standards for market conduct within the life insurance industry.

In the last 10 years, Dick has served as a case consultant and/or expert witness in a number of defense *and* plaintiff complaints involving life insurance sales. A case summary is available on request.

Dick's most current series of articles can be found in the Journal of the Society of Financial Service Professionals, where he writes about *Technology* and its effect on financial professionals.

This book, along with other books, is available at discounts that make it realistic to provide it as a gift to your customers, clients, and staff. For more information on these long lasting, cost effective premiums, please call us at (800) 272-2855 or you may email us at sales@fpbooks.com.